Ian McEwan was born in England in 1948 and began writing in 1970. He lives and works in London. His stories have appeared in *American Review*, *Transatlantic Review*, *Tri-Quarterly*, *Amazing Stories*, *Bananas*, *New Review*, *Encounter*, *Time Out*, *De Revisor* and *Avenue* (Holland) and *Nagy Vilag* (Hungary).

His first book, *First Love, Last Rites*, won the Somerset Maugham Award in 1976. This, and his second book, *In Between The Sheets*, are also published in Picador, together with his novels *The Cement Garden* and *The Comfort of Strangers*.

Also by Ian McEwan
in Picador

First Love, Last Rites
In Between The Sheets
The Cement Garden
The Comfort of Strangers

Ian McEwan

The Imitation Game

Three plays for television

published by Pan Books

All performing rights of these plays are fully protected
and permission to perform them, whether by amateurs or
professionals, must be obtained in advance from
Deborah Rogers Ltd, 5–11 Mortimer Street, London WIN 7RH.

This collection first published 1981 by Jonathan Cape Ltd
This Picador edition published 1982 by Pan Books Ltd,
Cavaye Place, London SW10 9PG
9 8 7 6 5 4 3
This collection © Ian McEwan 1981
ISBN 0 330 26830 9
'The Imitation Game' first published April 1980 in *Quatro*,
© Ian McEwan 1980
Filmset in Great Britain by
Northumberland Press Ltd, Gateshead, Tyne and Wear
Printed and bound by
Richard Clay (The Chaucer Press) Ltd, Bungay, Suffolk

for my parents,
David and Rose McEwan

Contents

Introduction

I first wrote a television play in 1974 because I wanted to break the isolation of writing fiction. I had no other job and I was far less reconciled than I am now to the essentially crackpot activity of sitting down alone several hours a day with an assortment of ghosts. I envied people who, even while they often complained about each other, collaborated, sped in taxis to urgent conferences; they appeared (I begin to doubt this now) saner and happier for having to do with each other. I thought of writing for television rather than for the stage because, like most people, I had spent far more hours in front of television sets than in theatres; I felt familiar with television's 'grammar', with its conventions and how they might be broken. As a short story writer I was attracted by its scale, its intimacy. The possibilities and limitations presented by the thirty, fifty, or even seventy-five minute television play seemed very close in some ways to those presented by the short story: the need for highly selective detail and for the rapid establishment of people and situations, the possibility of chasing one or two ideas to logical, or even illogical, conclusions, the dangers of becoming merely anecdotal.

Finally, television was, and is, dominated by the powerful, cohesive conventions of its naturalism. The programme-maker who departs radically from these conventions can be sure of at least irritating or surprising the audience – there is a base line of expectation. Literary fiction, on the other hand, as the older form, is not similarly dominated; there are authors writing comfortably inside the narrative conventions of the nineteenth century and publishing alongside writers of 'post-modernist' pastiches of eighteenth–century novels. Naturalism is the common language of television, not the language we speak, but one we are accustomed to listen to. Simply by association it has become the language of the State, of an illusory consensus, and prone to all its contradictions. The centrality of television naturalism suggested, or so I thought, that formal experiment could therefore really matter, that by calling into question the rules of the common language the viewer could be disoriented and tempted to regard the world afresh. These of course were grand expectations. The non-stop omnivorousness of television, aided by the tone of vacuous after-dinner chat of much television reviewing, tend to make such pronouncements of intent sound a little reedy.

Of the three plays printed here the first two were attempts, however weak, to kick over the traces. The third, 'The Imitation Game', is not formally experimental at all. I had begun to think there might be more effective, if well tried, means of trying to regard the world afresh.

'Jack Flea's Birthday Celebration' was written in 1974, shortly after I had finished writing the last of the stories that were to make up my first collection, *First Love, Last Rites*, and I think of this play as really belonging in that volume. It was commissioned originally by Barry Hanson, who was producing from Birmingham half-hour plays by new writers — hence the series title, 'Second City Firsts'. A standard procedure in the commissioning of a play, especially one by an unknown author, is for a synopsis to be written and then, once the producer is satisfied that the writer's 'idea' is sound and feasible, for a contract to be offered. It seemed to me a deadening process. I duly presented my 'idea', discussed it at length with the producer, signed a contract and wrote a play whose every line was still-born. Rewrites failed to rescue it. I explained to Barry Hanson that I could not know what I was writing about until I had written it. He promptly sent a second contract for a play entitled 'Blind Date', and encouraged by his willingness to take a chance on me I set to work. When Hanson left Birmingham, Tara Prem inherited the project. She and Pedr James, the script editor, made numerous suggestions for improvement and the play's final shape owes a lot to them.

My intention was to take a television cliché — a kind of

family reunion, a dinner party – and to transform it by degrees and by logical extension to a point where fantasy had become reality. The self-reflecting fiction at the centre of the play is perhaps one of those conceits that many writers new to a form are tempted to exploit. As it turned out it was not, as I had feared, too literary or undramatic. It simply became a feature of David Lee's illusory sense of control.

The play was helped enormously by the fact that the actors thought it very funny. Producing the play in Birmingham had one distinct advantage; at the end of a day's rehearsal the four actors – who all came from far away – could not go home. They had to hang about together in restaurants or in the hotel bar. No one could quite escape his or her part. By the end of ten days a very odd and gratifying level of controlled hysteria had been reached and this suited the claustrophobic nature of the play perfectly, as did the detached quality of Mike Newell's camera script.

I adapted 'Solid Geometry' in 1978 from the short story I had written in 1973. The story had very distinct origins. A mathematician friend from Chile had recently told me of a 'proof' for a plane without a surface and had outlined for me the consequences of such a proof being valid. Independently of this I had been reading Bertrand Russell's diaries and I wanted to write a story which would somehow illustrate the way diary writing, in its selectivity, closely resembles fiction writing. Thirdly, I wanted to write about the collision of two intellectual worlds. In 1972 I bought a bus in Amsterdam with two friends and travelled the hippy trail to Afghanistan and into the North West Frontier Province. During the preceding year in England and all along the route to Kabul I met people who spoke of the world in specifically anti-rationalist terms. The talk was of Alan Watts, Timothy Leary, Ken Kesey, Ouspensky, of bits and pieces of Jung, of the I Ching and the Tarot cards and of how psychotropic drugs, which we consumed in large quantities, might transform the mechanistic, aggressive world we had left behind into the peaceable kingdom. At the time it was a great liberation from a formal education that had seemed to have gone on too long

– I had finished a Master's degree the year before. When I returned to England, determined to carry on writing (I had published two stories by then), I found the cautious, analytical voices of a literary education vying with the intuitive and carefree. Albert and Maisie became the exaggerated representatives of each – the highly rational and destructive against the loving but self-deluded. The intended irony was that Albert uses the very system ('the mathematics of the Absolute') to dispose of her, that Maisie endorses and he has repudiated.

'Solid Geometry' is hardly a profound story. It is a little too neat, and at best simply clever. It gave me great satisfaction at the time because it seemed to tie up odds and ends that at one point seemed to belong to two or three stories. Its three-layered time scheme suggested that it might adapt well to television and I first suggested it to the BBC in 1975, but without success. Then early in 1978 Stephen Gilbert commissioned it for a series called 'The Other Side', also being made from Pebble Mill, Birmingham.

The immediate problem was to dramatize the relationship between Great-grandfather and Maxwell, which is merely reported in the story. It was also important to prevent Albert from becoming too sympathetic. It could easily happen because he is the one with the diaries, and through whom we have access to Great-grandfather, Maxwell and Vienna. Correspondingly, it was necessary to make Maisie as sympathetic as possible in her attempts to rescue the marriage; that way Albert's disposing of her would appear all the more callous. When the play went into production I discovered that dazzling electronic techniques were on hand not only for the paper flowers and Maisie's final disappearance, but also in moving us from one time level to another through the medium of a glowing page of the diary. The scenes of the mathematicians' conference in Vienna were to be shot through glass, a film technique adapted for tape.

After a week's rehearsal in March 1979 I began to think that this was, potentially at least, a far better play than a short story. It had a resonance and life that had not been present previously. The relationships between Maisie and Albert on the one hand, and Great-grandfather and Maxwell on the other, seemed to parallel and reflect each other. What was merely anecdotal in the story now seemed a strong narrative line. The mere cleverness of the story was easily displaced by the rapport between the two sets of actors, particularly between Mary Maddox and Clive Merrison.

On 20 March, four days before we were due to record the play in the studio, the BBC management called a halt to production; exactly why, and why we could not have been consulted first, I am unlikely now ever to discover. Mr Philip Sidey, Head of Network Centre, the administrative head of BBC Birmingham, objected strongly to the play, and Mr Shaun Sutton, Head of Drama Group, Television, effected the ban. At a meeting with the latter I was told the play was 'untransmittable' and that this was not a time for adventurous projects. Specific objections to the play were not mentioned then or at any other time during the minor storm that followed. While we were meeting, the BBC put out a press notice that announced the ban and referred to 'grotesque and bizarre sexual elements in the play'. The decision was presented as irrevocable. There could be no negotiation or compromise.

Naturally we would have resented compromise, but we were too deeply committed to the project not to explore every conceivable way of keeping it alive. For example, if the ban originated from a simple visceral response to a preserved penis in a jar, then we should have talked because there may have been room for manoeuvre. Who knows, if the contents of the preserving jar had been shrouded in murky liquid, its contents only to be glimpsed and guessed at, if it had been seen, once Maisie had broken the jar open, as undifferentiated grey tissue on Albert's desk, then it could have been effective enough for being inexplicit. It would have been immensely irritating to deal at such a trivial level, but worth it.

Again, if the objection was to the love/disappearance act at the end, then we certainly should have talked. Mary Maddox was to have played the scene naked, it is true, but nakedness is not new to television, and Mike Newell had yet to write his camera script. The camera has to be told how and what to look at. From the point of view of dramatic effectiveness discretion here was our best option; to have allowed the camera to become a *voyeur*, to have introduced at the climax of the play the self-consciousness of pornography, would have been completely diversionary.

But the BBC executives saw only a 'dirty' play and their mood was more retributive and paranoid than constructive. Stephen Gilbert, the producer, was sacked after publicly criticizing the ban. He was reinstated after a union-backed appeal but with severely reduced responsibilities. Gillian Reynolds, a 'Kaleidoscope' presenter, lost her job for writing about the ban in *Broadcast* magazine. Through a series of bungled or deliberately mismanaged statements from the BBC press office, 'Solid Geometry' became, for ten days or so, widely celebrated in the press as a play with bizarre sex scenes. Stephen Gilbert ascended to headlines as TV SEX BOSS (ON CARPET). I sped in taxis to urgent conferences. Then the whole thing was forgotten

I wrote 'The Imitation Game' less from a need to collaborate than from a sense of dissatisfaction with my fiction. My novel *The Cement Garden* was in certain respects a synthesis of some of the concerns of my short stories, and after I had finished it, in August 1977, I felt I had written myself into too tight a corner; I had made deliberate use of material too restricted to allow me to write about the ideas that had interested me for some years. The Women's Movement had presented ways of looking at the world, both its present and its past, that were at once profoundly dislocating and infinite in possibility. I wanted to write a novel which would assume as its background a society not primarily as a set of economic classes but as a patriarchy. The English class system, its pervasiveness, its endless subtleties, had once been a rich source for the English novel. The system whose laws, customs, religion and culture consistently sanction the economic ascendancy of one sex over another could be a still richer source; men and women have to do with each other in ways that economic classes do not. Patriarchy corrupts our most intimate relationships with comic and tragic consequences, and as a system it can be described in microcosm through its smallest and most potent unit, the family. *The Cement Garden* embodied something of this, and so did some of my short stories, particularly as parodies of male attitudes in 'Homemade' and 'Dead As They Come'. But my narrators were frequently too idiosyncratic or solipsistic to allow me the freedom to explore.

After eight months of writing notes and instructions to myself, and of false starts, I had found no way into the kind of novel I wanted to write. I worked on a short story about a man who lives in the American Mid-West (where I had been living) and who divides his time between looking after his daughter and polishing his performance of Mozart's Fantasia for piano, K475, a piece of music that obsessed me. Then Richard Eyre, who had just moved from the Nottingham Playhouse to the BBC, asked me to write a television play and I abandoned the story. I thought that by distracting myself, by doing something completely different, I could come back refreshed to my non-existent novel.

Initially I wanted to write a play about Alan Turing, the brilliant young mathematician who was brought to Bletchley Park from Cambridge during the war to work on Ultra, the decipherment of the German Enigma codes. He was one of the founding fathers of modern computers. He was a homosexual and suffered for it at the hands of the law. He died in 1953 in circumstances so far not completely explained.

I first heard of Turing in 1975 when I was writing a magazine piece on machine intelligence. Dr Christopher Evans of the National Physical Laboratories gave me an article by Turing, published in 1950 in *Mind*, entitled 'Computing Machinery and Intelligence'. In it he proposed the 'imitation game' as an operational procedure for approaching the question Can Machines Think? I heard more about the importance of Bletchley from Donald Michie, Professor of Robotology at Edinburgh University. Three years later I read Angus Calder's *The People's War*, a social history of World War II, and resolved to write something one day about the war. I come from an Army background and although I was born three years after the war ended, it was a living presence throughout my childhood. Sometimes I found it hard to believe I had not been alive in the summer of 1940.

But it was not at all easy to research either Bletchley or Turing's time there. A few books had been published, but there was a great deal of material that at that time (spring 1978) had not yet been released. I spoke to the historian Peter Calvocoressi who had been head of Air Ministry Intelligence and was well placed to write the history of the Ultra secret. He was frustrated by the lack of primary sources and said that if the papers were not released soon he would be too old to sift through them all and write his book. I spoke to Andrew Hodges who was writing Turing's biography. Reasonably enough he was reluctant to tell me facts that he had uncovered through painstaking research, but he told me enough about Turing's life and death to show me how little I knew. I had been researching for three months, and I knew that Turing would have to be invented.

And by this time certain other facts about Bletchley Park were interesting me more. By the end of the war ten thousand people were working in and around Bletchley. The great majority of them were women doing vital but repetitive jobs working the 'bombes' – electro-mechanical computing machines (Turing was a major force in their development) which were fed 'menus' and ran through thousands of combinations of letters until a code was broken. The 'need to know' rule meant that the women knew as much as was necessary to do their jobs, which was very little. As far as I could discover there were virtually no women in at the centre of the Ultra secret. There was a widely held view at the beginning of the war that women could not keep secrets.

Secrecy and power go hand in hand. Traditionally women had been specifically excluded from warfare, just as they had been excluded, by clearly stated rules written by men, from government, higher education, the professions, trade guilds, the priesthood and from inherited property; in effect, until recent times, from citizenship. And yet women seemed somehow essential to the conduct of war. Their moral and emotional commitment was vital, for they were the living embodiment of what the men fought to protect from the

Enemy. Their position was made more complex in modern warfare when sheer shortage of manpower impelled governments to bring women into the services. They were asked in not as fighter pilots or to mastermind intelligence operations, but as the housekeepers of war – cooks, chauffeurs, secretaries. In the Imperial War Museum library I came across the text of a wartime wireless broadcast – 'Henceforward, as our colossal war machinery gets underway, no skilled person is to do what can be done by an unskilled person, and no man is to do what can be done by a woman.'

When I began to speak to ex-ATS and WRNS the picture became even more complicated. Nearly all of them were now married women whose children had grown up and married. They had done the repetitive tasks connected with Ultra and then, bound by the Official Secrets Act for over thirty years, had spoken to no one about their work, not even their husbands. They spoke of the great camaraderie among the women which they felt – and this was said without bitterness – was incompatible with married life. Despite the hardships of military life, the crowded living quarters, low wages, lack of privacy, exhausting work, occasional bullying, the one word which recurred in their reminiscences was 'independence'. Without the war they would normally have expected to move straight from their father's house to their husband's. Despite the kinds of jobs assigned to them (I spoke to drivers and cooks as well as special operators) the war presented a unique and guiltless freedom from the strictures of family life, and from economic dependence on a particular man.

By this time I had come to think of Ultra as a microcosm, not only of the war but of a whole society. Peter Calvocoressi graphically described Ultra's organization on the 'need to know' basis as a set of concentric rings. The closer you moved to the centre, the more men you found; the further you moved to the periphery, the more women. By having a woman at the centre of the film (I no longer thought of it as a play) I could disguise my own ignorance about Ultra as hers. The idea was to have her move from the outermost ring to the very centre, where she would be destroyed. At the centre would be a sexual relationship; its misunderstandings would be the consequence of the absurdity of the structure. Turing by this time had disappeared and his place taken by Turner who anachronistically expounds the imitation game. Music – in its written form a kind of code – became important to the film, and the heroine inherited the Mozart Fantasia.

This was the novel I had wanted to write, and after I had finished the script there were times when I regretted intensely that it was a television film. These regrets disappeared as soon as I began to work with the director, Richard Eyre. I do not think a writer could have hoped for more sensitive, imaginative direction. It was, in effect, his first film too and this gave our collaboration during the year before going into production, and through rehearsals, shooting and editing, an open, exploratory quality that was thoroughly exhilarating.

I.M.
London,
February 1980

Jack Flea's Birthday Celebration

'Jack Flea's Birthday Celebration' was produced by Tara Prem and directed by Mike Newell, recorded at Pebble Mill, Birmingham, in January 1976 and transmitted, in the series 'Second City Firsts', on 10 April 1976.

Cast

David Lee	DAVID WILKINSON
Ruth	SARAH KESTELMAN
Mr Lee	IVOR ROBERTS
Mrs Lee	EILEEN MCCALLUM

1 Mr and Mrs Lee's House. Bedroom
Evening

MRS LEE, *a woman of about fifty, sits at her dressing-table, preparing herself for an evening out. She hums quietly. We see a powder-puff and much flesh.*

2 Ruth's House. David's Room
Same Time

DAVID LEE, *a young-looking twenty, rocks himself gently in a wicker hanging chair. He passes in and out of shot.*

3 Mr and Mrs Lee's House. Bedroom

In the dressing-table mirror we discern MR LEE. *He stares over his wife's shoulder.*

4 Ruth's House. David's Room

DAVID *crosses to a table and sits down in front of a typewriter.*
He types.

We see in tight close-up the title 'Jack Flea's Birthday
Celebration', typed in upper case.

We see DAVID's *hand pull the paper clear and set it down on a*
pile.

We pull back and see DAVID. *He contemplates the typewriter.*
From downstairs we hear the sound of tinny symphonic music from a
transistor radio, and RUTH *calling up to* DAVID *with increasing*
irritation.

He pays no attention.

5 Ruth's House. Living-room

A large living-room, tastefully sparse in decor. At one end a door to
kitchen. At the other a door to stairs. At the kitchen end of the room
a dining-table and four chairs. At the other end a couple of soft chairs
and a short settee. Spread about the floor is a vacuum-cleaner.

RUTH, *thirty-six, and at present bad-tempered, holds a kitchen*
sieve in one hand. With the other she is trying to disentangle the
vacuum-cleaner.

On one of the chairs is a magazine. On the arm-rest a beer can and
an empty glass and the small radio. The objects on the arm-rest
fall to the floor as she knocks into the chair. Radio goes off.

RUTH. David, David. They'll be here any minute.

6 Ruth's House. Kitchen

At the sound of sharp hissing she runs back into the kitchen. A complicated meal is in preparation. The scene is one of impenetrable chaos. Every available surface is taken up with saucepans, dirty plates, clean plates, vegetable peelings and so on. Two saucepans are boiling over.

RUTH *drops the sieve and lifts the saucepans off the stove. There is nowhere to put them down. She curses under her breath.*

The doorbell rings. RUTH *edges the saucepans among the debris on the table. On the far side a bag of flour tips to the floor. She changes her mind and puts the pans on the floor. She shouts with genuine fury.*

RUTH. David . . .

7 Ruth's House. David's Room

DAVID *remains perfectly still.*

8 Ruth's House. Front Porch

MR *and* MRS LEE *wait.*

RUTH's *voice.* David! Answer that bloody door.

MRS LEE *gasps quietly.* MR LEE *clears his throat.*

9 Ruth's House. Hallway

RUTH *strides to the door. A short pause as she adapts the expression on her face. She flings open the door.*

RUTH. Good, good, come in ... just ... that's right.

MR LEE. Thought we had the wrong house for a moment, ha ha ha.

MRS LEE. You said you were sure it was this one. *I* thought you were sure anyway.

RUTH. Leave your coats ... no ... yes, let me take them. That's right. David's upstairs. He'll be down. I'll give ... pardon?

MRS LEE. I said this *is* a warm house. Lovely.

10 David's Room

At the sound of his parents' voices DAVID *smiles faintly but does not move.*

11 Downstairs. Hallway

RUTH. Yes, I could ...

MRS LEE. I thought it was when we were coming down the path, I said that does look like a *warm* house. Didn't I.

MR LEE. Yes, yes. Yes.

RUTH. I could open a window. It does get a bit ...

MRS LEE. Oh no, no. Lovely the way it is. Just right.

MR LEE (*at the same time as his wife*). Yes, yes. I mean, or no. No. Ha ha.
RUTH. Good, then I'll just give him a call.
MR LEE. Good idea.

12 Living-room

By this time all three have stumbled into the living-room. MR *and* MRS LEE *hold the centre, almost back to back.*

RUTH *goes to the foot of the stairs and calls up in a parody of a polite coo.*

RUTH. David. Your parents are here.
MRS LEE. Mmm ... and we are looking forward to meeting .
RUTH. Oh yes, I'm sorry. I'm Ruth.

MR *and* MRS LEE'S *faint, nervous laughs and How-do-you-dos.*

RUTH. What can I offer you to drink?
MR LEE. Oh, ah, I'll ...
MRS LEE. What have you got?
RUTH. Whisky, sherry, beer.
MR LEE. Whisky.
MRS LEE. Sherry.
MR LEE. Yes, ha ha, sherry.
MRS LEE. Thank you.

The LEES *sit down stiffly on the edge of the settee.* RUTH *sits facing them. They all sip. A threatening silence.*

RUTH *offers crisps. The crunching is very loud.*

MRS LEE. Do you have a job, Mrs ...
RUTH. Ruth.
MRS LEE. Ruth?
RUTH. Yes, I'm a teacher.
MR LEE. I hope you've been teaching our David a ...
MRS LEE. Local is it, your school?

RUTH. Gas Road Comprehensive.
MRS LEE. Oh, so you don't have far to go, do you?
RUTH. It's pretty close.

13 Staircase

DAVID *is sitting halfway up staircase. He is listening to the conversation with horror and pleasure.*

MR LEE's *voice*. You get the 49 up Tavistock Hill.
RUTH's *voice*. I walk usually.

14 Living-room

MRS LEE. It's not far.
RUTH. No.

Another silence threatens. All three look to the door leading to the stairs.

MR LEE. Tavistock Hill though, that's a steep one isn't it?
RUTH. I don't go that way.
MR *and* MRS LEE *together*. No?
RUTH. I go another way.

A brief pause; all gulp their drinks.

MR LEE. What way's that then?
RUTH (*with an edge of panic*). Outside here I cross the road and go down Bluebell Lane, and then I turn right into Kabul Avenue till I come to the roundabout, straight over and down Rawalpindi Road, past the Lamb and Flag and into Khyber Pass Road and then down the pedestrian subway

under the bypass and along a path which comes out behind the Priory Road Garage, over the zebra crossing . . . and I'm there.

MRS LEE. Quicker that way I suppose.

RUTH (*desperate*). David! David!

DAVID appears immediately in the doorway.

DAVID. Hello Dad.

MRS LEE. David love.

DAVID shakes hands with his father and is embraced by his mother simultaneously.

RUTH. Where were you just now?

DAVID. I was in the toilet.

MRS LEE. Lavatory.

DAVID. That's right, Mum . . . I suppose you've . . Dad, Mum . . . Ruth. Ruth's a schoolteacher.

He sits next to RUTH.

MRS LEE. Gas Road Comprehensive.

RUTH. I've just been telling them.

Short pause.

MRS LEE. The Stokes's boy goes there. You remember the Stokes don't you, David?

DAVID. Nope.

MRS LEE. Well their boy goes there. Perhaps he's in your class.

RUTH. I've got thirteen classes.

MRS LEE. Black hair and . . . a very ordinary sort of face.

DAVID. You must know the one, Ruth.

RUTH. Does he play the French horn?

MRS LEE. Oh, I don't know. Does he, Henry?

MR LEE. I don't know who we're talking about.

MRS LEE. You know, the Stokes's boy.

MR LEE. Stokes?

DAVID's enjoyment of and RUTH's horror at following exchange.

MRS LEE. You remember. They gave us a lift in their car.

DAVID. Don't they drive an A40?

MR LEE. You mean Mike and Frieda Summers.

MRS LEE. That was before Christmas. I'm talking about just the other week.

MR LEE. I haven't been in a car for months.

MRS LEE. Oh Henry! What about yesterday then?

MR LEE. Yesterday? Yesterday? That was a taxi.

MRS LEE. What a memory.

RUTH. I am sorry. I've let your glasses get empty.

MRS LEE. He forgets what day of the week it is, you know.

MR LEE. I've never in my life forgotten . . .

MRS LEE. It'll be his own name next.

MR LEE. There's a difference between a car and a taxi, isn't there, David?

DAVID. Course there is, Dad.

RUTH. Mrs Lee, another sherry? Or perhaps you need something stronger?

MRS LEE. Oh yes, I'd . . . you know . . . love . . .

RUTH. Sherry for you then. Mr Lee, why not try a Scotch this time.

MR LEE. Scotch, yes.

15 Living-room
A Minute or so Later

They all have their drinks. A thin attempt to begin again.

MR LEE. Well, David, here's to you, and a very ha ha happy birthday.

RUTH *and* MRS LEE. Happy Birthday.

DAVID. Thank you.

MRS LEE *knocks back her sherry in one gulp.* RUTH *reaches over and instantly, with a certain malice, fills her glass.*

MRS LEE. Ooo! Look at me.

RUTH. Never mind.

MR LEE (*looking significantly at his wife*). Well I think we could, you know, give David his ... don't you?

MRS LEE. It's only a little thing, mind. It's so difficult to know what to get you nowadays.

She reaches into her handbag and brings out a small box. From where he is sitting DAVID *can reach the gift as it is held out to him. This he tries to do. But his mother wants him to come closer. She draws her hand back a little.* DAVID *gets up and goes over to her.*

MRS LEE. Happy birthday, David.

MR LEE. Happy birthday. It should be of some use to you. I've never seen you with any before.

DAVID. Thanks, thanks a lot.

MRS LEE *tilts her face to be kissed.* DAVID *looms over her awkwardly, pauses and then bends down and pecks her lightly on the cheek. As he is straightening, his mother pulls him down again, kisses him on the lips and gives him a brief, tight hug.* RUTH *watches with poorly concealed horror.* DAVID *meets* RUTH's *eye. Unobtrusively he wipes his lips and opens the box. Inside is a pair of cufflinks.*

DAVID. Cufflinks ... very nice, thanks Mum, thanks Dad.

He shows them to RUTH. MRS LEE *gets out of her chair and begins to roll down the sleeve of* DAVID's *ragged denim shirt.*

MRS LEE. Look at the state of this shirt. Worn to nothing it is.

MRS LEE *reaches for the cufflinks but they are now in* RUTH's *hands. Without deliberately appearing to,* RUTH *moves in such a way that the box is out of* MRS LEE's *reach. Then* RUTH *takes one of the cufflinks out of the box and clips it into the sleeve that* MRS LEE *has rolled down. To do this she moves in between* MRS LEE *and* DAVID, *with her back to* MRS LEE. MRS LEE *tries to move round to the other sleeve but again she is blocked.* RUTH *rolls down the other sleeve and pins it. This is all done with a certain drunken sway. And with the pretence that it is not being done anyway.*

RUTH (*as to a small child*). There. Smart boy now.

DAVID. Yes.

MR LEE. Very smart.

MRS LEE. Let me see. One of them's in the wrong way. The initial faces outwards doesn't it, Henry?

MR LEE. Oh yes, yes. Definitely outwards.

MRS LEE. Come here, David, stand still, there, that's better.

RUTH. Do you think he'll be able to put them on himself?

MR LEE. Ha ha ha.

DAVID. I expect I'll manage.

MRS LEE. You may well laugh. He was twelve years old and still getting his shoes on the wrong feet.

DAVID (*a little desperately*). Some people don't know what's right from what's ... left.

MR LEE. Ha ha ha, that's a good one that is.

MRS LEE (*motherly pride*). *And* sleeping with the light on when he was fourteen.

RUTH. And even now he still wets the –

DAVID. Another drink? Dad, a Scotch? Good. Mum, rum? Then we can start on the wine.

MRS LEE. Oooo, wine, lovely.

MRS LEE *goes into peals of giggles.* DAVID *is stooped over a low table pouring a drink.* RUTH, *standing up now, tousles* DAVID's *hair. He inclines a little towards* RUTH's *breasts and for a brief moment rests his forehead there.*

Fade.

16 Living-room
Half an Hour Later

DAVID *and his father.* RUTH *and* MRS LEE *are in the kitchen. The level in the Scotch bottle considerably down.* MR LEE *is attempting a 'man to man' chat with* DAVID. *He has a cigar to help him. An unanswered remark appears to hang in the air with the smoke.* MR LEE *goes to speak.* DAVID *looks up.* MR LEE *looks down.* DAVID *looks away.*

MR LEE (*glance to kitchen*). But you can't just ...
DAVID. I'm not.
MR LEE. Why don't you get yourself ...
DAVID. I don't want one.

MR LEE *smiles weakly and retreats behind his cigar.*

17 Kitchen

RUTH *is busy with the meal.* MRS LEE *is appraising the mess and beginning to clear some of it up. They hear the murmur of conversation from the living room.*

MRS LEE. What a lovely bowl.
RUTH (*pushing past*). Excuse me.
MRS LEE. Pity it's got that crack.
RUTH. David did that. Mind.
MRS LEE. I'm in the way, aren't I? Is this the drying-up cloth?

RUTH *is attending to the conversation next door.*

DAVID'S *voice.* No ... why shouldn't I, anyway? Separated
    actually ...

RUTH *snatches up a bowl of peanuts and hurries into the living-room.* MRS LEE *trails behind.*

DAVID. ... No, thirty-six ...
RUTH. David's writing a book. Hasn't he told you about it yet?
MRS LEE. A book! I didn't know you were writing a book.
    What sort of book, dear?
DAVID. I am not writing a book.
RUTH. He's got his own little room upstairs. It's a novel, isn't
    it, David?
DAVID. No.
MRS LEE. What's it about?
DAVID. Nothing.
MR LEE. Sounds interesting.

RUTH. It's about a little boy who runs away from home.
DAVID. No it isn't.
RUTH. Yes it is. I think you should tell your parents all about
it.

DAVID *sighs*.

MRS LEE (*proudly*). He's shy.
MR LEE. Come on, David.
RUTH. Why don't you read some out to them. You know
they'd be very interested.
MR LEE. Course we would.
RUTH. Especially your mother.
MRS LEE. What?
DAVID. It's of no interest to anyone.
RUTH. Don't be silly. Of course it is. And anyway, I think it
would be very unfair not to tell your mother about it.

She touches DAVID'*s shoulder.*

MRS LEE. Unfair?
RUTH. Go on.
MR LEE. Don't spoil the party, David.
MRS LEE. Why would it be unfair not to tell me? (RUTH *smiles*)
Why, David?
DAVID. Don't listen to her.
MRS LEE. I'm not ... (RUTH'*s smile broadens*) in it or something?
RUTH. Ask David.
MRS LEE. Well, David?
DAVID. It's got nothing to do with anyone.
MR LEE. If your mother's in it then it's got something to do
with her, hasn't it.
DAVID. I never said she was in it.
MRS LEE. If I'm in something then I've got a right to know.
Haven't I, Henry? Haven't I got a right?
MR LEE. Of course, dear. Every right.
MRS LEE. If I'm in it I want to see it. I won't look at the other
bits, I promise you. Just the bits with me in.
MR LEE. That's fair.
RUTH. Come on, David. Give us a reading of work in
progress.

DAVID. Balls.

MRS LEE. David!

DAVID. Listen. You don't put people *in* novels, you draw on your . . .

MRS LEE. You just go and get that thing and read it to us and mind your language.

MR LEE. Yes, you do as you're told for once.

DAVID. All right. If that's what you want, if that's what you really want.

DAVID *gets to his feet unsteadily as he speaks. All four have boozed enough now to take risks, but they are still clear-headed.*

18 Living-room

DAVID *sits with a large folder in front of him. It is arranged in such a way that no one else can see what he is reading. Everyone is sitting down. The drink goes round.*

DAVID. This chapter's called 'A Birthday Celebration'. But first you better have the story so far. (*Parodic story-so-far voice*) Our young hero, Jack Flea . . .

MRS LEE. Jack Flea?

DAVID. . . . Jack Flea has run away from home to escape his miserably ineffectual father and the stifling, sinister attentions of his mother, Mrs Flea. Out of the frying-pan though, for he finds himself living with Hermione, a woman nearly twice his age, a woman obsessed by the two great failures in her life. The first to have a child, the second to achieve an orgasm. Of the second she has wisely despaired, but of the first . . .

RUTH. David . . .

MRS LEE. Sshhh . . .

DAVID. . . . er, she decides to make Jack Flea her child, her fantasy child. It's a role that poor Jack Flea cannot resist. Hermione becomes his fantasy mother and to get a clearer perspective on it all he decides to write a novel about himself. (*Pauses. Looks up*) Now in this novel he wants to write a scene where his mother, his real mother and his fantasy mother meet. Well, instead of trying to make it all up he invites Mr and Mrs Flea round to meet Hermione. It's his birthday anyway, see. That way the chapter will write itself, or so he thinks. So . . . 'A Birthday Celebration'. (DAVID *clears his throat conspicuously*) 'The doorbell rang. It was them. Hermione was still upstairs painting over the cracks in her face. (MRS LEE *suppresses a snigger*) Jack showed the Fleas into the living-room. They sat down. There was an uneasy silence. Jack Flea looked across at his mother, at that pasty, familiar face, at the surplus skin hanging from her face in obscene folds. My God, he thought to himself, but you're ugly . . .'

MR LEE *breaks into wild, uncontrollable laughter. It drowns out the narrative.* MRS LEE *is furious with both son and husband, and uncertain which to go for first.* RUTH *smiles faintly.* MRS LEE *pummels her husband.*

MRS LEE. Stop it, stop it, stop it, stop.

MR LEE *staggers through the door to the stairs, still laughing.*

MRS LEE *snatches the piece of paper out of* DAVID's *hands. It is completely blank.*

MRS LEE. Ooo David!

From the stairs MR LEE *cackles helplessly.*

RUTH (*cool*). I think we had better begin the dinner.

19 Living-room

The four sit round the table. From where he sits DAVID *pours the wine.* MRS LEE *is still furious with everyone.*

When MR LEE *goes to speak only a high-pitched squeaking sound comes out. He clears his throat noisily.*

MR LEE. Well now ... it's ... er, it's a long time since you sat down to a meal with your mother and I (*Silence*) ... isn't it, David?

DAVID. Yes, Dad.

MR LEE. Isn't it, love?

MRS LEE. Is it?

MR LEE. And yes, now I come to, ha ha ha, think of it, I can't even remember the last time. (*Silence*) Can you, David?

DAVID. Nope.

MR LEE. Was it, no, no, it wasn't ... er ... can you, love? Love?

MRS LEE. What?

MR LEE. Remember, you know, ha ha ha, the last time.

MRS LEE. No I can't.

MR LEE. Oh. Ha ha, no one can remember. Er David, would you pass me the salt.

DAVID. Yes Dad.

He makes no move.

MR LEE. David?

DAVID. Oh yes, sorry.

DAVID *seizes the wine bottle and fills his father's glass.*

MR LEE. No, no, thanks anyway, but I wanted, yes, that, the salt.

DAVID. This? This is the pepper.

MRS LEE. The salt is next to your plate.

MR LEE. Oh yes, it almost bit me, look ... ha ha ha ...

No one laughs. MR LEE *subsides, defeated.*

20 Living-room
A Couple of Minutes Later

DAVID *and* RUTH *are in the kitchen seeing to the next course.*

MR LEE *tops up his wife's glass. She looks away. He tries to take her hand across the table. She withdraws her hand.*

MR LEE. A good dinner, eh? Tasty, not as tasty as the ones you ... but a very nice house, er very nice, especially those curtains over there. Have you seen curtains like that before? Very unusual. Indian, I expect...

MRS LEE. Oh Henry!

MR LEE. ... or Chinese I mean. (*He leans over the table and takes her wrist firmly*) I know what you're thinking, dear, I know you think that when David read out that bit about ... er ... Mrs Flea's ... dead ... skin ...

By clenching his teeth MR LEE *is able to hold back the laughter that threatens to obliterate his apology.*

MR LEE. I wasn't (*clench*) laughing, at you. No. (*Pauses*) I mean, not Mrs Flea, no, no ... no.

MRS LEE. What were you laughing at then?

Very shakily MR LEE *gets to his feet and walks round the table.*

MR LEE. I wasn't laughing, you see.

MRS LEE. Not laughing?

MR LEE. I mean I was, I was just ...

MRS LEE. Just?

MR LEE. I wasn't really laughing, I was laughing to myself, I was ... (*He rests his head on his wife's lap*) ... drunk.

MRS LEE *strokes his head and smiles.*

MRS LEE. Drunk, were you?

MR LEE. I wasn't laughing, you see.

MRS LEE. I see.

21 Kitchen

RUTH *and* DAVID *are conspicuously not talking.* RUTH *takes an apple pie from the oven.* DAVID *brings a jug of cream. They stop in the entrance to the living-room.* MR LEE *still kneels with his head in his wife's lap, muttering something inaudible.*

RUTH. Oh.

MRS LEE *glares at* RUTH *with intense hostility.* MR LEE *starts and scrambles to his feet, still muttering. On his way up he bangs his head on the corner of the table, a resounding blow which knocks a few things to the floor.* MRS LEE *gives a little scream.* DAVID *laughs.* MR LEE *tries to ignore the blow. He staggers towards* RUTH *and* DAVID *with the air of one who believes he is behaving with impeccable calm.*

RUTH. Oh.
MR LEE. Just talking, you know, and, ha ha ha, admiring your curtains. Let me take that for you.

He seizes the large oven dish from RUTH's *hands. She is wearing oven gloves.* MR LEE *breaks into a run towards the table with the dish.*

MRS LEE. Don't put it down there, love. You'll burn the table.

MR LEE *puts the dish on the floor.*

DAVID. It'll burn the carpet.

MR LEE *picks up the dish and runs back towards* RUTH. *But she has taken off her gloves.* MR LEE *turns and runs towards the window.*

MRS LEE (*finds a table mat*). Put it down here, Henry.

MR LEE *changes direction again and bangs the dish down on the table.*

MR LEE (*concealed agony*). Delicious. It looks delicious. But heavy.
MRS LEE (*looking angrily at* RUTH). Did you burn your hands dear?

MR LEE. Oh no, no, not really.

MRS LEE. She should've given you the oven gloves.

MR LEE. I never wear gloves . . . ha ha ha, always losing them.

22 Living-room

They are all seated. RUTH *serves large portions of pie.* DAVID *pours wine. A short silence.*

MRS LEE *glances sideways at* RUTH *before speaking.*

MRS LEE (*slyly*). So . . . er . . . you never wanted to have children of your own then, Ruth?

RUTH. Oh yes, I've always loved children. Especially little boys.

MRS LEE. Do you regret, you know, not having them?

RUTH. I used to.

MRS LEE. It's not what everybody wants, is it?

RUTH. Just as well, some women make dangerous mothers.

MRS LEE. You don't want children now then?

RUTH. I'm quite happy now.

MRS LEE. I mean, having David was the greatest thing in my life. He was a lovely child, you know, beautiful to look at. And we were very close, weren't we, David?

DAVID. Can't remember.

MRS LEE. Do you remember that lovely holiday we had in Torquay?

DAVID. Nope.

MRS LEE. You were only eighteen months. We had a very nice bed and breakfast almost on the sea front with a flagpole in the garden and the landlady . . .

MR LEE. Mrs O'Malley.

MRS LEE. Malone.

MR LEE. Malone.

MRS LEE. Mrs Malone had a daughter, about fourteen she was. Do you remember her?

DAVID. No.

MRS LEE. Oh, she took a great liking to you, she did.

MR LEE. A great liking.

MRS LEE. She used to take you for walks, get you your tea, change you, put you to bed, play with you for hours and hours ... don't you remember her?

DAVID. No.

MRS LEE. I didn't mind at first. She was a nice girl, very careful, you know. And it kept you out of trouble.

MR LEE. And it gave us a free hand.

MRS LEE (*turning to* RUTH). But you see, by the end of the first week he thought *she* was his mum. He was calling her Mummy and crying when she went off to school in the morning. He wouldn't have anything to do with me.

MR LEE (*points with his spoon*). You really upset your mother then, David.

MRS LEE. He wouldn't let no one else put him to bed. Only her. He wouldn't let no one else feed him with his spoon. Only her.

MR LEE. Very upset she was.

MRS LEE. There was nothing for it. We had to find another bed and breakfast. What a scene that was. The girl crying. You screaming Mummy. The whole street out watching, I'll never forget that, never. Don't you remember any of it, David?

DAVID. No.

MRS LEE (*reaching into her handbag, which is on the floor by her chair*). I found a picture from that holiday, the other day, I'm sure you'd like to see it. (*Showing it to* RUTH) Me on the beach, look, with David in my arms. See, a lovely little boy he was. We were very close, you can see how close we were.

MRS LEE's *Torquay story is designed to get at* RUTH *and succeeds. Throughout it we see* RUTH's *stony reaction.*

While the photograph is still being shown to her, RUTH *gets up and stands behind* DAVID's *chair. She brushes the hair from his eyes in a motherly way.*

RUTH. Now he's *my* lovely little boy.

She reaches down for DAVID'S *napkin and fixes it around his neck like a bib. She takes his spoon out of his hand. While she speaks she feeds* DAVID *mouthfuls. Her tone is mischievous, paying off a score. All by now should be well and truly boozed.*

He doesn't let anyone else feed him with his spoon. It has to be me. He doesn't let anyone else put him to bed. Only me. We're very close. You can see how close we are.

MRS LEE. He might be living with you but he's still my son.

RUTH. No, no. He's my little boy now. I'm his Mummy now. I play with him for hours and hours, I take him for walks, I give him his tea, I change him, I tuck him up at night. Sometimes he comes and curls up in my lap and closes his eyes and I feed him milk (MRS LEE *gasps*) ... from a baby's bottle ... yes, my little Jack Flea sucks and remembers he's only a tiny little boy, my little boy. And you know one day I'm going to buy him a big playpen so he can't run away ... because little boys sometimes run away, and I'll keep him all mine, he'll never leave the house, he'll be mine, all mine.

RUTH *helps* DAVID *to eat with his spoon. Then he eats on his own.*

He offers a heaped spoonful to his mother and she swallows it. He throws a spoonful in his father's face. RUTH *smacks him and he drops the spoon. He starts to cry and nuzzles against* RUTH. *Imperceptibly his crying and her comforting noises turn to laughter.*

MR *and* MRS LEE *are still stunned, then, slowly, they get the joke. They are infected by the laughter.*

To show that she is not put out by RUTH'S *charade,* MRS LEE *picks up the spoon and feeds* DAVID. *The laughter redoubles.*

MR LEE. ... in a ... in a playpen, David in a ...

MRS LEE. ... on his lap ... I thought ... I thought she meant ...

MR LEE. I can just see our David ... in a ... a play ... a playpen ...

MRS LEE. ... fed him milk ... I thought ... she ... she ...

MR LEE (*recovering a little*). What a turn, eh? What a turn. Jack Flea ...

23 Living-room
Several Minutes Later

A record is playing. DAVID *is dancing with his mother,* RUTH *with* MR LEE.

Ad libbed *birthday toasts, shouts etc. Brandy slops into glasses.*

Fade to RUTH *dancing with* DAVID, MR LEE *with* MRS LEE. *Hooting, staggering.*

Fade to all four, arms on shoulders and swaying to drunken snatches of 'Auld Lang Syne'. They link hands in a circle.

24 Hallway

MR *and* MRS LEE *are putting on their coats. Farewell bluh and yawning. A knock at the door.*

MR LEE. . . . 's our taxi.

They crowd into the open doorway. A strained formality is back with them. They all seem to sober up. DAVID *stands behind* RUTH.

MRS LEE. Oh, it *is* a warm house. You can tell as soon as you step outside.

MR LEE (*shaking* DAVID's *hand*). Well, David, try and keep in touch a little more. You know how your mother worries.

DAVID. Yes Dad.

MRS LEE. Goodbye, Ruth. It was a lovely dinner. Feel bad that I didn't help you tidy.

RUTH. Oh, no, no . . .

MRS LEE. Anyway, we'll have you round to us one of these days.

RUTH. I'll look forward to that.

MRS LEE *leans forward to give* RUTH *a peck on the cheek, but* RUTH *extends her hand at the same time.* MRS LEE *grasps it awkwardly with her left hand.*

DAVID *submits to a kiss from his mother.* RUTH *shakes hands with* MR LEE. *The taxi-driver clears his throat noisily. Goodbyes and waving. The front door closes.*

RUTH *and* DAVID *smile at each other.*

RUTH. Let's go to bed.

25 Living-room

We inspect the remains of the birthday party: an empty bottle of Scotch, a half-empty bottle of Scotch, an empty sherry bottle, wine bottles, a few records out of their sleeves on the floor, untouched portions of apple pie, DAVID's 'bib' *next to an overflowing ashtray.*

26 Bedroom

Close-up of DAVID *in bed, eyes closed.* RUTH *leans forward and they kiss deeply.*

RUTH (*whispers*). Go to sleep now.

DAVID *goes to speak.* RUTH *shushes him.*

We pull away and see that DAVID *is lying in a large cot.* RUTH *in a nightdress slides the side up, goes to the door, pauses there a moment to look at* DAVID, *smiles to herself, turns the light out and softly closes the door.*

A small night-light burns.

Credits.

Fade out.

Solid Geometry

'Solid Geometry' was produced by Stephen Gilbert and directed by Mike Newell, at Pebble Mill, Birmingham. The production was halted on 22 March 1979.

Cast

Albert	CLIVE MERRISON
Maisie	MARY MADDOX
Great-grandfather	DENYS HAWTHORNE
Maxwell	JOHN FORTUNE
Auctioneer	JIM BROADBENT
Hunter	MICHAEL HARBOUR
Mathematician	JACK HOLLOWAY
Goodman	BLAIN FAIRMAN
Old Man in Conference Hall	WILL HORTON

1 1875. A Country Auction Afternoon

A lull between bids. Among the small crowd of men grouped near the AUCTIONEER's *lectern we find but do not linger on* MAXWELL *and* GREAT-GRANDFATHER.

MAXWELL *is in his mid-forties. A self-taught man, a poseur, self-consciously a 'man of the world' whose essential innocence alongside* GREAT-GRANDFATHER's *looks like urbanity. That is why* MAXWELL *needs him.*

GREAT-GRANDFATHER *is a little older. A man of rabid, shifting enthusiasms whose intelligence far outstrips his wisdom. A compulsive theorizer who has experienced very little of the world outside his study. That is why he needs* MAXWELL.

The AUCTIONEER's *gaze combs the room.*

AUCTIONEER. Have all the ladies now departed from the sales room? Have ... Yes? Very well then, gentlemen, we may begin. Gentlemen, if you please

Two assistants stand on either side of the AUCTIONEER, *each holding a sealed glass jar. The* AUCTIONEER *gestures left.*

AUCTIONEER. This anatomical curiosity, gentlemen, was once the living property of one Captain Nicholls who died in Horsemonger Jail in 1835. I have it on absolute authority that the good, late doctor severed the part only *minutes after death*, not, as wild, irresponsible rumour puts out, minutes before. And thus you see it, gentlemen, preserved for the furtherance of natural science and the edification of medical students.

GREAT-GRANDFATHER *and* MAXWELL *edge their way to the front of the crowd.*

It measures a little under twelve inches and, as you may observe, gentlemen, it is in a beautiful state of preservation.

A most virtuous and scientific item. The bidding starts at ten shillings.

GREAT–GRANDFATHER, *wild and boyish, is now at the front of the crowd, right beneath the lectern, straining forward to examine the penis in the jar.*

MAXWELL *stands a little behind him, hand touching his shoulder as if to restrain him.*

G.-GF. Look at that, Maxwell! Wonderful, quite wonderful. I must have it.

The AUCTIONEER'*s point of view:* GREAT–GRANDFATHER'*s eager, upturned face.*

G.-GF. Three guineas!

The crowd murmurs.

MAXWELL. My dear friend, not so quickly.
AUCTIONEER. Three guineas, I hear three guineas, three guineas, three guineas, four guineas, four guineas . . .
G.-GF. Seven guineas!

Ad lib *bidding to fourteen guineas.*

G.-GF. Eighteen guineas!
AUCTIONEER. Eighteen guineas, I hear eighteen, eighteen guineas, eighteen, eighteen guineas, eighteen, eighteen, eighteen guineas . . . sold to the gentleman in front of me.

GREAT–GRANDFATHER *embraces* MAXWELL.

AUCTIONEER. Passing to the item on my right; delicacy, gentlemen, inhibits a full description. The . . . unnamed portion of the late Lady Barrysmore, secured and preserved by the family physician with the permission of her closest relatives.

GREAT–GRANDFATHER *and* MAXWELL *have moved across to examine the second jar. Unlike the first its contents cannot be seen. The liquid is too murky.*

G.-GF. Maxwell, what an excellent set the pair would make.
MAXWELL. I'm not so certain.

AUCTIONEER. A priceless item with aristocratic connections, the bidding commences at five guineas.

G.-GF. It can be none other than the female counterpart to Captain Nicholls.

MAXWELL. I urge you not to bid.

AUCTIONEER. Five guineas, five guineas...

G.-GF. I see them now, side by side above the fireplace.

GREAT–GRANDFATHER *tries to raise his arm to attract the* AUCTIONEER's *attention.* MAXWELL *restrains him.*

MAXWELL. It's badly preserved, whatever it is, and therefore quite worthless.

G.-GF. But the set, Maxwell, the set.

MAXWELL. Please take my advice. It's badly done, utterly worthless.

Long shot. MAXWELL *ushers the protesting* GREAT–GRANDFATHER *through the crowd.*

Ad lib *bidding has proceeded meanwhile to thirty guineas.*

AUCTIONEER. Thirty guineas, I am bid thirty guineas. Thirty, thirty, thirty guineas ... and sold to our dear friend Mr Sam Israel. A handsome acquisition, sir.

2 Great-grandfather's Study Evening

Book-lined, book-strewn. A clock ticks heavily. A coal fire burns in the grate.

GREAT–GRANDFATHER *eats alone at a table set in the centre of the room.*

3 Great-grandfather's Study
Later

GREAT–GRANDFATHER *sits at his writing-desk. A couple of*
mathematical treatises lie open next to a sealed jar. He turns a
leather-bound diary to a fresh page and writes.

G.–GF. (*voice over*). 10 October 1875. This morning I read with
great pleasure Mr Malthus's pamphlet of 1798 entitled 'On
the Principle of Population'. I find I am in a position (*pauses*
and glances round the room) to endorse wholly his
conclusions. During the afternoon, in the company of my
beloved friend M, I attended the auction at Melton
Mowbray and there purchased the most extraordinary
thing ...

Voice fades. The open pages of the diary glow. Surrounding objects
darken.

4 The Same Diary
A Different Table
One Hundred Years Later
Very Early Morning

Bird song and distant traffic. We pull away from the diary and
discover the apparatus of scholarship – card indexes, reference
volumes, a typewriter, a jar of pencils and pens – and a great
number of similar diaries set with their spines upright along the back
of the table, ranging (the dates inscribed upon the spines) from 1865
to 1899.

We see the penis in the jar catching the early morning sunlight and we become aware of MAISIE's *voice from the bedroom next door. She is muttering in her sleep.*

Pulling steadily away from the table, we see the study, the austere, bare floor. MAISIE's *nightmare mutterings become desperate shouts.*

5 Bedroom. Semi–darkness

MAISIE *wakes from her nightmare, sits up and turns on the light.* MAISIE *is in her late twenties, a product and to some extent a victim of the Sixties – unfocused ambitions, reflective in a self-destructive way. But she has warmth and must by sympathetic.*

At her side, lying on his back with his eyes closed is ALBERT. *Thirtyish, self-absorbed, somewhere in his mind he has left his wife far behind. Eerily cold.*

MAISIE *attempts to pull* ALBERT's *arm free of the bedclothes and drape it round her shoulders,* ALBERT *is not helpful.*

ALBERT. What now?
MAISIE. It was a terrible dream. A nightmare.
ALBERT (*without opening his eyes*). Really?
MAISIE. It was the one I had before. I was in a plane flying over a desert. But it wasn't really a desert. I made the plane go lower and I could see there were thousands of babies heaped up, stretching away to the horizon, all of them naked and climbing over each other. I was running out of fuel and I had to land the plane. I had to find a space, I flew on and on, looking for a space.

No reason to believe that ALBERT *is listening to this. His eyes remain closed throughout. At the end of* MAISIE's *speech he makes no response.*

It was so frightening, Al.

ALBERT *yawns and turns on his side.*

ALBERT. It was only a dream. Go to sleep now.
MAISIE. No! I daren't go to sleep, not just yet.
ALBERT. Well, I have to go to sleep. I have to get up in an hour.
MAISIE. Please don't go to sleep yet. Don't leave me here.
ALBERT. I'm in the same bed for Chrissakes.
MAISIE. Please don't leave me awake, please don't leave me awake.

ALBERT's *eyes close.*

6 Bathroom
   Day

ALBERT *sits on the lavatory, fully dressed. On his knees he balances a hardcover journal in which he is making a diary entry. He pauses. The bath tap drips.*

He continues to write.

7 Living-room
   Day

MAISIE *sits in a yoga position.*

8 Albert's Study
Day

ALBERT *is at his desk sorting through one of his card files. He picks out one of the diaries, dated 1877, and by referring to the card file finds the page he wants. We read:*

> *3 June. Tuesday, and as usual, my dear friend M to dinner.*

The page glows whiter . . .

9 The Same Diary on Great-grandfather's Writing-desk
Evening

Across the room in armchairs are CREAT-GRANDFATHER *and* MAXWELL, *lighting after-dinner cigars.*

MAXWELL (*a little drunk, a little pompous*). I'm something of a scholar myself, in these matters at least – as all men-of-the-world should be.

G.-GF. Maxwell, your erudition in a number of fields is a constant source of surprise and pleasure to me.

MAXWELL. Experience untempered . . . unseasoned . . . by serious reflection and scholarship counts for nothing in the end, a hollow sham.

G.-GF. You put it nicely.

MAXWELL. So I am able to inform you with considerable authority that the Church has always taken a dim view.

G.-GF. Of course.

MAXWELL. Theodore, the seventh-century theologian . . .

G.-GF. Ah yes, Theodore!

MAXWELL. Theodore believed it a sin equal to . . . self-abuse . .
G.-GF. Onanism!
MAXWELL. Precisely, and therefore worth forty penances.
G.-GF. Indeed, but for which particular transgression?
MAXWELL. My dear friend! For proceeding with a member of
the fair sex . . . *a posteriori.*
G.-GF. Of course, I had quite forgotten.
MAXWELL. However, and this is my point . . .

*There is a knock at the door. The two men become immobilized
mid-gesture.*

MAISIE's *voice.* How's it going? I've brought you some tea.

We pull away to find the diary on GREAT–GRANDFATHER's *desk. In
the background the two men, out of focus.*

MAISIE's *voice.* It's Earl Grey, your favourite.

10 The Same Diary on Albert's Desk
Day

ALBERT (*without turning round*). Oh, yes. Great. Put it there.
MAISIE. I've made a cake too.
ALBERT. Oh.

MAISIE *sets down her tray on the floor behind* ALBERT *and kneels
down beside it. She cuts the cake and hands* ALBERT *his tea.*

MAISIE. How are you getting on?
ALBERT. All right.
MAISIE. Solved the mystery of Maxwell's disappearance yet?
ALBERT (*through a sigh*). Nope.
MAISIE. Very strange, vanishing just like that. Perhaps he
smoked too much opium. I had this dream last night that
was very strange too. I was trying to fly this plane over a
kind of desert, only it wasn't really . . .

ALBERT. Maisie, not now. Can't you see I'm in the middle of something here.

MAISIE *leaves the study in silent fury.* ALBERT *takes a slice of cake and returns to the diary.*

11 The Diary. Great-grandfather's Study

G.-GF. Of course, I had quite forgotten.

MAXWELL. However, and this is my point, advanced scientific opinion on the Continent poses a contrary attitude and insists that *a posteriori* is the most *natural* way.

G.-GF. Indeed.

MAXWELL. And once more the Church is wholly discredited by Science. As evidence, the scientists cite, in the first instance, the position of the clitoris itself.

G.-GF. A very good point!

MAXWELL. And in the second, the preferred method of all other anthropoids. They *all proceed a posteriori.*

G.-GF. Remarkable. (*Stands*) An appropriate moment, Maxwell, to show you some calculations I have made since our last conversation. You will remember that it was my ambition to illuminate what is most obscure in human nature and conduct with the penetrating light of mathematics, that most severe taskmaster of all our knowledge, the foundation of all sciences, the finest, most elevated and noble of ...

MAXWELL. Yes, yes.

G.-GF. (*produces a fat sheaf of mathematical calculations*). What less irrelevant then, what more obscure in human conduct than the very act of procreation itself. Given the human form – an irregular lamina which I have expressed in algebraic and geometric terms – and given the spatial alignments prerequisite to the act of generation – which I have translated into a set of *simultaneous* equations – and given the arc of movement each limb may make at its respective joint . . .

MAXWELL. Yes, given all that.

G.-GF. What then are the maximim number of positions in which the act of love may take place? And how may these be expressed mathematically?

MAXWELL. But . . .

G.-GF. This first section demonstrates, by reduction to absurdity, that there can only be a prime number of positions.

MAXWELL. But my dear fellow . . .

G.-GF. And the second proves beyond all doubt that the prime number concerned is seventeen.

MAXWELL *breaks into uncontrollable laughter. We pull away.*

12 Albert's Study

ALBERT *closes the diary and stands.*

13 Living-room

We take a long look at MAISIE. *She sits cross-legged on the floor. She finishes rolling a joint. Spread out in front of her is a Tarot card reading. She inhales, considers the cards, exhales.*

ALBERT *appears behind her, pausing to watch briefly and scornfully. As he passes (*MAISIE's *point of view), he treads on a couple of the cards.*

14 Bathroom

As before, ALBERT *sits on the lavatory fully dressed, writing in his journal. The bathroom door-handle turns.* MAISIE *knocks, gently at first.* ALBERT *goes on writing.*

MAISIE. How long are you going to be?
ALBERT. Not long.
MAISIE. Open the door. I need to get in there.
ALBERT. You'll have to wait.
MAISIE (*shouting*). Let me in. You're not using the toilet.
ALBERT. Wait.
MAISIE (*kicking the door*). My period has started. I need to get something.

ALBERT *continues to write. Silence now from the other side of the door.* ALBERT *finishes.* MAISIE *is waiting for him outside the bathroom.*

15 Landing

MAISIE *hits him over the head with the heel of a shoe.* ALBERT*'s ear is cut.*

MAISIE. Now we're both bleeding.

She steps round him into the bathroom and slams the door.

16 Albert's Study

ALBERT *finds a tissue for his ear.*
The diary glows . . .

17 Great-grandfather's Study

MAXWELL *laughing.*

18 Landing

ALBERT *waits, shoe in one hand. With the other he nurses his ear.*

Cut to another shot of the same ... time passes.

When MAISIE *finally steps out* ALBERT *catches her on the top of the head with the shoe with far greater force and accuracy than she hit him.*

MAISIE *stands still, determined not to appear hurt. But there is a pause before she can speak. She stares at* ALBERT, *who wilts perceptibly.*

MAISIE. You worm!

19 Great-grandfather's Study
Evening

MAXWELL *finds his voice through his laughter.*

MAXWELL. Seventeen ... seventeen ... excuse me. Scholarship without experience, on the other hand ...
G.-GF. Could you but understand mathematics.
MAXWELL. Travel to our great capital, inquire of the professional ladies who nightly patrol the Haymarket and

without hesitation they will tell you 'Forty-eight, and if it pleases you to step this way, sir . . .'

G.-GF. Heaven forbid.

MAXWELL. As for the scholars, well there's a Mr Forberg who has accounted for ninety positions, and Romano, a pupil of the distinguished Raphael, has made twenty-six different drawings.

G.-GF. (*leafing through his papers*). There could be errors in calculation, or something I failed to take into account.

GREAT-GRANDFATHER *crosses the study and sets his papers down on the writing-desk. The diary (and the sealed jar) is in shot.*

MAXWELL (*as we close in on the diary*). Mathematics is, as you say, a pure and noble pursuit, and your own genius is beyond question. But my dear fellow, passion won't be reduced to numbers. it simply won't go . . .

MAXWELL's *voice fades.*

20 Albert's Study

ALBERT *closes the diary and puts it in its place alongside the others. He contemplates Captain Nicholls.*

21 Living-room
Evening

MAISIE *is sitting in an armchair eating her supper. The floor is littered with Tarot cards and books on mysticism.*

ALBERT *enters with his own plate of food and makes his way to a second armchair.*

MAISIE. Don't kick my cards all over the place. You could try walking round them, you know.

ALBERT (*knocking a couple of* MAISIE's *books off the armchair*). You could try putting the bloody things away for once.

MAISIE. I'm halfway through a very important reading. And don't throw my books around like that.

ALBERT. A very important reading!

MAISIE. You'd go crazy if I treated your books like that.

ALBERT. Do you really think this junk is going to sort you out? (*Poking at a card with his foot*) Hanging from a tree by one leg strongly recommended.

MAISIE. Don't be pathetic.

ALBERT. It beats me how a grown person can take this nonsense seriously.

MAISIE. As a matter of fact . . .

ALBERT. I suppose one consolation is that you'll be 'into' something else soon. Not so long ago you were a dedicated ecologist preparing to save the planet. Before that you were in touch with flying saucers and before that you were a trainee psychotherapist. What's next? Witchcraft?

MAISIE (*brave pretence at calm*). It so happens that the Tarot cards are a very ancient system of knowledge which embodies a complete representation of the unconscious.

ALBERT. Amazing, and the whole thing fits in your back pocket.

MAISIE. Centuries of intuitive knowledge held together in a system.

ALBERT. Intuitive knowledge! In other words mumbo jumbo.

MAISIE. A man locked in a cell with only the Tarot cards would have access to all knowledge.

ALBERT. All knowledge?

MAISIE. Provided he knew how to use the cards, yes.

ALBERT. So using the cards properly could he work out the street plan of Valparaiso?

MAISIE. Now you're just being stupid.

ALBERT. Could he find out the best way to start a laundry business? The best way to make an omelette or a kidney machine?

MAISIE. You're so predictable, you're such a drag.

ALBERT. Could he work out why Maxwell disappears from the pages of my great-grandfather's diary?

MAISIE. You're so narrow. Can't you see those are not necessary things?

ALBERT. They are still knowledge. Could he find them out?

MAISIE (*pauses*). Yes, he could.

ALBERT *breathes deeply, smiles and goes on eating.*

MAISIE. What's so funny?

ALBERT *shrugs.* MAISIE's *exasperation mounts.*

MAISIE. Why did you ask all those pointless questions?

ALBERT. I dunno really. I just wanted to know if you really meant *everything.*

MAISIE (*shouting*). Damn you! Why are you always trying me out? Why can't we have a real conversation about something?

ALBERT *shrugs. Both retreat into bitter silence and continue to eat.*

22 Stables

GREAT-GRANDFATHER *is bent over an elaborate, heavy, brass-knobbed press which has a pressure gauge. On the floor a bucket of horse dung.*

GREAT-GRANDFATHER *makes calculations, consults notes.*

MAXWELL *appears behind him.*

G.-GF. (*without turning round*). I wonder if you remember, Maxwell, a conversation we had several weeks ago. You had just returned from one of your trips to London and you informed me of the extent to which the thoroughfares were fouled by horse dung.

MAXWELL. Yes, damn nuisance it is too.

G.-GF. The general consensus there, so you said, was that certain streets could be totally impassable before long.

MAXWELL. That's what the cabbie said who drove me through Mayfair on the way to lunch with Lady Mortimer ...

G.-GF. I've gathered certain useful statistics concerning the metropolitan equine population and, following the principles of the great Malthus, have assumed a geometric growth in that population ...

MAXWELL. Good Lord!

G.-GF. And after a careful study of a street plan of the city – help me with this lever – and these experiments to determine the compressibility of the material in question – there, that should do it – I shall be in a position to demonstrate to the world, through the medium of my pamphlet entitled '*De Stercore Equorum*' and by mathematical calculation, that the streets of our beloved capital ...

MAXWELL. Which you have never yet visited.

G.-GF. And never shall – will be utterly impassable by the year 1935. All commercial, artistic and domestic life will be brought to a standstill, the great, good heart of our empire shall cease to beat, the ...

MAXWELL (*taking* GREAT-GRANDFATHER's *elbow*). My dear friend, perhaps the time has come for me to tell *you* my own story of mathematics, and of a mysterious, quite unbelievable event. I have held back this last year from telling you, preferring to wait for my moment, and now ...

G.-GF. Now indeed, Maxwell! But surely not here in my stables. If it's mathematics and mystery then we must treat the story-teller with some respect. Let me make you comfortable in my study with a bottle of my best claret and, if you require it, a little opium ...

They leave and GREAT-GRANDFATHER's *voice fades. The sound of a door opening. A sudden draught blows* GREAT-GRANDFATHER's *forgotten calculations to the floor.*

The door slams shut.

23 Albert's Study
Dawn

Dissolve to one of the diaries on ALBERT's *desk. Bird song and distant traffic. Sounds, as before, of the gathering momentum of one of* MAISIE's *nightmares.*

24 Bedroom

ALBERT *turns on the light.* MAISIE *sits up dazed.* ALBERT *gropes for his glasses.*

ALBERT. Tell me something, Maisie. What is it you really want? Why don't you go back to your job for Chrissakes? All these long walks, self-analysis, sitting around the house, lying in bed all morning, the Tarot pack, the nightmares .. I mean, what is it you want?

MAISIE (*wearily*). I want to get my head straight.

ALBERT. Your head, your mind, it's not like some old coat-hanger you know, that you can just bend into the right shape. It's more like a river, moving and changing all the time. And you can't make rivers flow straight.

MAISIE. Let's not go through all this again. I'm not trying to make rivers flow straight. I'm trying to get my mind straight.

ALBERT. But you've got to do something. You can't do nothing. Why don't you go back to work? You never had nightmares when you were working, you were never as unhappy as this when you were working.

MAISIE. I've got to stand back from all that. I'm not sure what any of it means any more.

ALBERT *gets out of bed and begins to dress.*

ALBERT. Fashion, that's all it is, fashion. Fashionable metaphors, fashionable reading, fashionable *malaise*. What do you care about Jung, for example? You've read twelve pages in a month.

MAISIE. Don't say any more. You know it leads nowhere.

ALBERT (*he has rehearsed this speech carefully*). You've never been anywhere, you've never done anything. You're a nice girl without even the blessing of an unhappy childhood. This bed-sit mysticism, joss-stick therapy, none of it's yours, Maisie, you've worked none of it out for yourself. You fell into it, that's what you did. You fell into a swamp of respectable intuitions. You haven't got the originality to intuit anything for yourself beyond your own unhappiness. Why are you filling your mind with other people's mystic banalities and giving yourself nightmares?

MAISIE (*close to tears, fighting them down*). And why are you trying to make things worse for me? Why do you have to go on and on and on? I feel like you're screwing me up, you know, like a piece of paper.

Pause. ALBERT *is tying his shoe-laces.* MAISIE *is sweetly conciliatory.*

MAISIE. Come over here, Al. Come and sit here. I want to touch you. I want you to touch me . . .

ALBERT *leaves the bedroom with a business-like sigh.*

25 Albert's Study
Fifteen Minutes Later

ALBERT *sits down at his desk with a cup of coffee. The diary in front of him glows . . .*

26 Great-grandfather's Study

Moving away from the diary we find GREAT-GRANDFATHER *and* MAXWELL *passing an opium pipe between them. A slow-motion, soporific feel about this scene.*

GREAT-GRANDFATHER *fills* MAXWELL'*s glass.* MAXWELL *settles back in the armchair, eyes half-closed. The room is lit principally by the light of the fire.*

MAXWELL (*remotely, hesitantly at first*). I've kept this story to myself for fear of appearing foolish in the telling ... but ...

G.-GF. But now you may feel secure before a bigger fool!

MAXWELL. My dear friend ... You remember that during my journey across Europe last year I visited Vienna.

G.-GF. Indeed. You gave a glowing report of it.

MAXWELL. What I omitted to tell you was that there came into my possession certain papers which claim – and only *claim*, mind you – to invalidate everything fundamental to our science of solid geometry, and in so doing undermine the whole canon of our physical laws ... forcing us, in short, to redefine our place in nature's scheme.

G.-GF. A modest enough claim.

MAXWELL. The author of these papers is – or should I say *was* – an obscure young mathematician from the University of Edinburgh, David Hunter. He had arrived in Vienna to read his thesis at an international conference on mathematics. But it was not Hunter who gave me the papers. They were entrusted to me by another young mathematician, an American by the name of Goodman. You'll recall that I corresponded with his father over a number of years in connection with his cyclical theory of menstruation, which is still largely discredited in this country.

G.GF. Because it's poppycock, that's why.

MAXWELL. All the same, the young Goodman, in a state of considerable agitation, gave the papers into my care with instructions that I was to deliver them to David Hunter if I was ever to learn of his whereabouts. Goodman planned to return to America the following day even though the conference had hardly begun. At first he would not tell me why he was leaving so soon, nor would he explain what it was that so greatly disturbed him. But then, and only after much persuasion and insistence on my part, he described what he had witnessed on the third day of the conference.

GREAT-GRANDFATHER *has relit the opium pipe.* MAXWELL *pauses to receive it. As* GREAT-GRANDFATHER *offers the pipe and* MAXWELL *stretches out his arm to take it . . .*

MAISIE's *voice.* What about you, then?

MAXWELL *and* GREAT-GRANDFATHER *remain fixed in their positions.*

ALBERT's *voice.* What?

27 Albert's Study

Through the medium of the diary we are back in ALBERT's *study.* ALBERT *raises his head, dazed.*

MAISIE *stands in the doorway in her dressing-gown. The penis floats unconcernedly in its jar.*

MAISIE. I said, what about you, then? What is it *you* 'really want'? Books! Crawling over the past like a fly on a turd.
ALBERT (*rallying*). Crawling, yes. But at least I'm moving.
MAISIE. You can't even speak to me. All you can do is play for points.
ALBERT (*turning his back on her*). Maisie, go away please.

MAISIE *hesitates, hurt, and leaves, slamming the door hard.*

ALBERT *returns to the diary.*

28 Great-grandfather's Study

MAXWELL *takes the pipe and draws deeply. When he begins to speak again we dissolve slowly into ...*

29 The Great Hall, Vienna

Where the mathematicians meet. A long polished table, strewn with papers, etc. The mathematicians seated around it applaud soundlessly under MAXWELL'*s words. A colleague stands, a sheaf of papers in his hands, and bows.*

We find HUNTER *among the mathematicians – wild, abstracted, Beethovenish look – barely remembering to clap.*

Huge double doors are flung open and liveried lackeys wheel in refreshments.

MAXWELL (*voice over*). The conference assembled every morning at nine o'clock. A paper was read and a general discussion ensued, followed by ovations and official citations. Now, the conference lasted two weeks and, by a long standing arrangement, the most eminent read their papers first, followed by the slightly less eminent and so on, descending through the hierarchy. Hunter was young and virtually unknown outside his university and he was placed to read on the penultimate day of the conference, by which time most of the important mathematicians would have returned to their respective countries. Hunter, however, was determined to be heard.

Sound up. The applause fades into a low hum of conversation. The mathematicians, many of them old and frail, rise slowly from the table. Coffee is offered round by the lackeys.

HUNTER *makes his way to the head of the table.*

HUNTER. Gentlemen ... gentlemen ... gentlemen, please. Gentlemen, I must beg you to forgive this irregular form of address. I promise I shall not keep you long. (*Holds up a sheaf of papers*) Rather than read my proofs to you, I will simply announce their conclusions. Gentlemen, my field is solid geometry. I have discovered, and I have effected, the plane without a surface.

The mathematicians, vaguely annoyed at having their refreshment time broken into, are now faintly amused.

HUNTER *takes from his pocket a piece of paper and begins to make rapid folds and incisions. Very tight shot of his fingers working at incredible speed.*

HUNTER. Bear with me ... it will take less than a minute ... now ... there.

What he has now resembles a paper flower. He holds it up and slowly turns it inside out. It glows brightly for an instant and then, slowly, disappears.

Pause. Silence. The mathematicians freeze into a tableau.

HUNTER (*very softly*). Behold, gentlemen, the plane without a surface.

Heavy silence.

MAISIE's *voice.* What are you reading?

All the mathematicians, HUNTER included, drop their guise and become interrupted actors. They turn towards the door.

30 Great-grandfather's Study

Dissolve to MAXWELL and GREAT-GRANDFATHER, who also look up suddenly and turn towards the door.

MAISIE's *voice.* Albert?

31 Albert's Study

Dissolve to ALBERT, *who looks up from the diary and turns towards the door.* MAISIE *leans there seductively. She has spent time on herself – 'Laura Ashley' clothes, newly washed and combed hair, etc.*

She crosses the room and stands behind ALBERT'*s chair. She massages his neck.*

MAISIE. What are you reading that's so interesting?

ALBERT. Some pages in the diary I've never seen before.

MAISIE. Didn't you hear me calling you?

ALBERT. No.

MAISIE. I was in the bedroom.

ALBERT. Ah.

MAISIE (*mouth close to* ALBERT'*s ear*). I was waiting for you. I called and called, and waited and waited. Now I've come to get you myself. I'm going to carry you off to bed ... mmm ... I'm going to have my way with you.

ALBERT. Oh.

MAISIE. I want you, Al. Do you know how long it is since we made love?

ALBERT. Yes.

MAISIE. Three weeks. Three whole weeks, Al. If you won't take me, then I shall take you. I love you. I *want* you. I'm sorry about this morning. I was being silly. Come with me now, we'll make it all right again.

ALBERT (*without turning round*). You know how it is ... with my work ... I don't ...

MAISIE. Come on.

ALBERT. No.

MAISIE *straightens and takes her hands off* ALBERT. ALBERT *tenses, waiting. He cannot quite see her.* MAISIE *picks up Captain Nicholls from the table. She tilts the glass and contemplates the drifting contents.* ALBERT *waits.*

MAISIE (*pauses*). You're so complacent!

She dashes the glass jar against the table.

ALBERT. No!

The penis lies across one of the diaries surrounded by broken glass and formaldehyde.

ALBERT (*slight whine*). Why did you do that? Why did you do that? That belonged to my great-grandfather. Maisie, why?

MAISIE. I'm going out for a walk.

She leaves. ALBERT *contemplates the huge, grey, slug-like thing. He picks pieces of glass out of his lap.*

32 A Plot of Earth

ALBERT *buries a small paper parcel. Sounds of close busy traffic.*

33 Albert's Study

ALBERT *dabs with his handkerchief at the formaldehyde on the diaries. A large, jagged lower portion of the jar to remain on his desk.*

He contemplates the diary. It glows ...

34 Great-grandfather's Study

The pipe is alight again. MAXWELL *draws.*

G.-GF. And then?

Dissolve to the Conference Hall.

35 Conference Hall

Still the heavy silence.

All the mathematicians stare at HUNTER. *We take a close look at their faces. In each one we see an almost imperceptible flickering and trembling, a tension of mounting fury expressed in total silence.*

Finally, one thin gasp escapes, and then another.

MATHEMATICIAN (*close to apoplexy*). How ... dare you, sir!
  How dare you insult the dignity of this assembly with a
  worthless conjuror's trick. (*Murmurs of assent*) You should
  be ashamed, young man, thoroughly ashamed.

With the exception of the servants who stand stiffly to attention with the refreshments, and of GOODMAN, *the young American, the whole room now erupts. The mathematicians advance on* HUNTER *shaking their fists, shouting insults and threats. Some bang the table in fury, others rip up conference papers.*

An old man reaches HUNTER, *stands on tip-toe to shake his fist under* HUNTER's *nose and drops to the floor clutching at his heart.*

HUNTER *remains perfectly still – a faint smile. When at last he raises his hand the mathematicians fall silent immediately. Under all this rage, they long desperately for an explanation.*

HUNTER. Gentlemen, your concern is quite understandable.
  Therefore I will effect another proof, the ultimate proof for
  which I require the services of an assistant.

Silence. GOODMAN *steps forward.*

GOODMAN. Stephen Goodman, Harvard, at your disposal, sir.
HUNTER. Thank you. Now . . .

HUNTER *strides through the crowd to a low chaise-longue which lies
against one wall.* GOODMAN *walks behind him; the rest follow more
slowly.*

HUNTER. I want you to take these papers with you when you
return to England . . .
GOODMAN. But I . . .
HUNTER. Keep them with you until I come to collect them,
or you hear of my whereabouts.
GOODMAN. But I am returning to the United States . . .

HUNTER *has turned to examine the couch and does not hear.*

HUNTER. Now I shall place myself face downwards here.
When my legs are raised you will take my ankles in your
left hand and with your right . . .

Long shot. The mathematicians are gathering round the couch.

HUNTER *gives his instructions to* GOODMAN. HUNTER *removes his
jacket and shoes and loosens his collar. He lies on the couch and with*
GOODMAN'*s help puts his body through a series of contortions.
These must seem improbable — use tight close-ups and other people's
legs!*

GOODMAN *begins to pass* HUNTER'*s legs through the hoop* HUNTER
has made behind his back with his arms. As he does so, HUNTER
disappears bit by bit.

The mathematicians are stunned.

HUNTER'*s voice (resounds).* Behold, gentlemen, the plane
without a surface.

A mathematician peers under the couch. Another looks in the folds of
HUNTER'*s jacket.*

Uproar.

Dissolve to GREAT–GRANDFATHER'*s study.*

70

36 Great-grandfather's Study

G.-GF. (*standing, excited*). And you have those papers, Maxwell!

MAXWELL (*sleepily*). I've had them for over a year now. I've written to the University at Edinburgh but the authorities there are not helpful. They say Hunter is on extended leave, and they will not divulge his address.

G.-GF. I insist you send for those papers immediately. I must see them.

MAXWELL. It's late, my friend. I will have them brought to you in the morning, I promise you. (*Yawning*) But be warned, I've been through those papers myself a number of times and there is simply no sense to be had of them.

G.-GF. You underestimate me.

MAXWELL. If there is anything there I am certain you are the man to find it. I've a strong suspicion though that Goodman was playing a practical joke on me. It could be his father put him up to it. Yes ... paying off an old score, or ... well ... you simply cannot trust Americans.

MAXWELL *falls asleep.* GREAT-GRANDFATHER *paces the study.*

37 Great-grandfather's Study

GREAT-GRANDFATHER *sits at his desk writing in his journal. Behind him* MAXWELL *sleeps.*

38 Great-grandfather's Study Morning

GREAT-GRANDFATHER *is at his desk surrounded by pages of* HUNTER's *thesis. He copies symbols on to the pages of the diary.*

Holding those symbols, we dissolve to ALBERT's *study.*

39 Albert's Study

ALBERT *slowly turns the pages of the diary. Each page is crammed with mathematical calculations. At the bottom of one proof he reads the words, 'dimensionality is a function of consciousness'.*

He turns more pages. More calculations. Then he reads, 'It disappeared in my hands!' On the next page a set of paper-folding drawings, each one numbered in succession. On another page is a set of numbered yoga positions. He stands suddenly. His chair tips over behind him.

Cut to ALBERT *rummaging through a drawer for a compass and a steel ruler.*

Cut to ALBERT *sharpening a pencil to a very fine point.*

ALBERT *has cleared a large space on his desk. He has arranged the steel ruler, compass and a Stanley knife neatly to one side of a clean sheet of paper. He consults the diary, makes a measurement and trims the paper.*

ALBERT *stands on the far side of his study contemplating the paper 'flower' on his desk. It is surrounded by shreds of paper.*

ALBERT *at his desk. Holding the flower, he consults the diary. He uses his thumbs to push the flower inside out. Nothing happens.* ALBERT *gasps, screws the flower up and hurls it at the floor. We see then ten similar screwed up paper flowers.*

40 Hall, Outside the Closed Door of Albert's Study

MAISIE, *dressed in overcoat and thick scarf, pushes open the door. She sees, as we do,* ALBERT *staring at his empty hands.*

MAISIE *takes a couple of steps into the room.*

41 Albert's Study

ALBERT *is too absorbed and does not look up.*

MAISIE. What are you doing?

ALBERT *starts. He picks up the broken piece of jar. He stares at* MAISIE *with growing resentment.*

ALBERT. Why did you do it?

MAISIE. Albert! You haven't been sitting there all afternoon thinking about that.

She stands by ALBERT'*s desk.*

What happened to it anyway? Did you eat it?

ALBERT. I buried it in the garden.

MAISIE (*kneeling by* ALBERT'*s chair*). Listen love, I really do feel bad about what happened and I'm sorry. I just sort of did it before I knew what was happening. One second it was in my hands, and the next ... I know it was important to you and I am really sorry, really I am. Will you forgive me?

ALBERT (*hesitates, then smiles*). Yes, of course I forgive you, Maisie.

MAISIE. Al!

ALBERT. I mean, it was only a prick in a pickle, wasn't it?

They laugh and kiss.

MAISIE. I love you, Al.

ALBERT. Mmmm.

MAISIE. I just know those diaries are going to be a great success when they're published.

ALBERT. Never know your luck.

MAISIE. And then we'll be able to go on holiday.

ALBERT. Somewhere cold, clean and treeless.

MAISIE. Or a hot, dirty jungle.

ALBERT. Separate holidays perhaps.

They laugh and kiss again.

MAISIE. Tell you what. I'll make a delicious dinner. Are you hungry?

ALBERT. Yes. That would be lovely.

MAISIE. And I'll get some wine.

ALBERT. Good.

She kisses him on the top of the head and leaves. As soon as she has gone ALBERT *returns to the diary.*

42 Bedroom. Day

ALBERT *carefully lays a fire – criss-crossing kindling on the crumpled remains of his paper flowers.*

43 Great-grandfather's Study Evening

We find a few empty wine bottles.

GREAT-GRANDFATHER *and* MAXWELL *are drunk. They are laughing helplessly.* GREAT-GRANDFATHER *is dividing his attention between helping* MAXWELL *undress and clearing a settee of books and papers.*

MAXWELL. You've advanced ... you've advanced ... this is one step forward from measuring the compressibility of horse dung.

G.-GF. It's a thousand steps forward. Now, off with these ... and this.

MAXWELL. Doesn't it require some faith on my part?

G.-GF. No, only on mine.

They collapse towards the settee laughing. GREAT-GRANDFATHER *disentangles himself.*

Now, to work, to work.

Again, helpless laughter.

44 Albert and Maisie's Kitchen Evening

ALBERT *and* MAISIE *are seated at a small table in a corner. They have finished eating. One bottle of wine stands empty and they are starting on another.*

ALBERT *has just finished rolling a joint. He lights up, inhales and passes it to* MAISIE.

MAISIE. There was a time when we did this every night.

ALBERT. And we were never out of bed before midday.

MAISIE. Remember that weekend when we smoked a whole ounce of grass.

ALBERT. A different world.

MAISIE. But we're not so different, I mean, underneath it all.

ALBERT. Certain things never change.

They hold each other's eyes for a couple of beats. ALBERT *pours more wine into* MAISIE's *glass.*

MAISIE (*fondly*). Here's to us then.

ALBERT (*fondly*). No, here's to *you*.

MAISIE. All right, to me.

She reaches across the table and strokes the side of his face. ALBERT *smiles and kisses her hand.*

ALBERT. You know, my great-grandfather once worked out by mathematics that there were only seventeen positions for making love in.
MAISIE. We've proved him wrong in our time, haven't we?
ALBERT. Certainly have.
MAISIE. And we still can.
ALBERT. We just need to get on top of our differences.

They laugh.

45 Kitchen
Half an Hour Later

The second bottle of wine is finished. So is the joint.

MAISIE. Next summer I'm going to work in Scotland for the Forestry Commission.
ALBERT. You said that last year ...
MAISIE. Yeah, but this year I'm really going to do it. Think of it, Al! Out working all day among trees, surrounded by mountains, getting into the land. Getting physically strong and suntanned. Listen, Al. Why don't we both go?
ALBERT. I've never thought about it.
MAISIE. It would be amazing, the two of us. You will have finished the diaries by then. The big outdoors, Al. Just think of us there, together.
ALBERT. It might do our marriage some good.
MAISIE. It's bound to ... all that space, those huge skies. We're so cramped here. We need to do something together, we need an adventure.

ALBERT. I'm convinced, you've sold it to me. Let's go up there together.

ALBERT *and* MAISIE *embrace.*

MAISIE. Oh Al, I'm so drunk, so stoned, so happy!

46 Bedroom

What takes place now between ALBERT *and* MAISIE *must look as much as possible like a scene of lovemaking.* MAISIE *lies face downwards,* ALBERT *lies beside her, caressing her back.* MAISIE's *words are blurred and luxurious. She is very relaxed, just as he intended. Only imperceptibly does he begin to arrange her limbs into the position he wants.* MAISIE *submits easily, wishing to abandon herself utterly to the moment . . . until it is too late.*

MAISIE. I was walking along the river this afternoon. The trees are beautiful now, the oaks, the elms . . . mmm . . . there are two copper beeches about a mile past the footbridge, you should see them now . . . ahh, that's nice . . .

ALBERT *kisses the nape of her neck and slowly brings her arms behind her back.*

There are blackberries, the biggest ones I've ever seen, growing all along the path, and elderberries too. I'm going to make some wine with them next year.

ALBERT *positions* MAISIE's *arms. His hands travel down her legs.*

And the river is really still. You know, reflecting the trees, and the leaves are dropping into the river. I found this little secret place, we should go there before the winter comes. It's a bed of leaves, and no one would ever find it.

ALBERT *slowly works* MAISIE's *legs upwards to form a hoop with her hands.*

I sat in this place for half an hour without moving. I was like a tree. I saw a water rat running along the opposite bank, and different kinds of ducks landing on the river and taking off. Ah! position number eighteen.

They laugh. ALBERT *kisses* MAISIE *and at the same time lifts her head backwards towards the hoop made by her legs and arms.*

I saw these two beautiful orange butterflies. They almost landed on my hand. Then ... careful. (*Shouting*) Careful! Al! That hurts!

ALBERT *begins to turn* MAISIE *inside out. All the while he continues to kiss her.* MAISIE's *groans suggest the abandon of lovemaking, as well as fear and pain.*

MAISIE. What's happening to me? (*Sighs*) Oh God, what's happening?

MAISIE *begins to disappear.*

MAISIE's *voice* (*very remote*). Al, where am I? ... Al?

Cut to ALBERT *sitting on the edge of the bed. A faint grin which does not part his lips.*

47 Great-grandfather's Study

GREAT-GRANDFATHER *sways slightly before the empty settee.*

G.-GF. Maxwell? Where are you, Maxwell? ... Maxwell?

Credits.

Fade out.

The Imitation Game

'The Imitation Game' was produced and directed by Richard Eyre, filmed on location in Essex and Suffolk in October and November 1979 and transmitted. as a BBC 'Play for Today', on 24 April 1980.

Cast

Cathy Raine	HARRIET WALTER
Anna Raine	LORNA CHARLES
Tony	SIMON CHANDLER
Tony's Mother	KRISTINE HOWARTH
Mr Raine	BERNARD GALLAGHER
Mrs Raine	GILLIAN MARTELL
Factory Clerk	KEITH MARSH
ATS Officer	PATRICIA ROUTLEDGE
Mary	BRENDA BLETHYN
ATS Sergeant	CAROL MaCCREADY
First Recruit	ANNIE HAYES
Second Recruit	JEAN LEPPARD
ATS Girl	PENNY SMITH
ATS Lance Corporal	SUE GREENWOOD
Sarah	BELINDA LANG
Dispatch-rider	DANIEL WEBB
Publican	PETER SCHOFIELD
Commanding Officer	TIM SEELY
Voice on Wireless	PETER CELLIER
Officer in Mess	ALISTER CAMERON
Turner	NICHOLAS LE PREVOST
Clark	KEVIN ELYOT
Matthews	MATTHEW SCURFIELD
Smith	JOHN GRILLO
Junior Officer	ANDREW SEEAR
Officer in Teleprinter Room	RHYS MCCONNOCHIE
Colonel in Cell	GEOFFREY CHATER

1 Early Summer 1940. Living-room Day

The modest, suburban home of the Raines, on the edge of a small southern town.

Late morning sunshine. The windows are open, the lace curtains stir in a light breeze.

Distant sounds of children at play. Bird song. The occasional passing car.

CATHY RAINE *sits at an upright piano, staring at the music in front of her.*

CATHY *is nineteen, intelligent, watchful. Her quietness masks her competitiveness. Under pressure from her father, she waits to be 'directed' into war work. A local munitions factory will open soon.*

With a pencil she marks the music. She positions her hands and takes a deep breath – a sense of beginning again for the hundredth time.

She plays – as in all other instances – Mozart's Fantasia, K475.

> *Title Credit.*

She falters. She rises impatiently.

She stands by the open window.

She crosses the room slowly, placing one foot directly in front of the other in order to delay her arrival at the mirror.

CATHY *stares at herself. She stands sideways on, trying to catch her profile.*

Somewhere in the house a door slams.

CATHY *moves away from the mirror.*

She sits in an armchair, a book in her lap.

2 Cathy's Bedroom
Day

It is a room cluttered with the layered accretions of childhood. Teddy bears, dolls, books.

CATHY *combs and pins her sister's hair.* ANNA *is about fifteen years old.*

From downstairs the sound of kitchen clatter and a wireless.

ANNA. . . . I want to see my hair. Are you doing it like last time?
CATHY. Exactly like last time.
ANNA. Do you think it's too long?
CATHY (*yawning*). No.
ANNA. My friend Sue at school, you know, Sue Morely, well she's had her hair cut really short and she's been growing it since she was six. And you know . . .
CATHY. She burst into tears when the hairdresser swept her hair into the dustbin.
ANNA. How did you know?
CATHY. I guessed.
ANNA. She felt as if she was saying goodbye to her childhood.
CATHY. Tragic.
ANNA. Shall I do yours now?
CATHY. If you want.

They change places.

ANNA. The factory opens next week.
CATHY. I know.
ANNA. Lucky you. Sue Morely's sister's going to be working there too. Three pounds ten a week. Making shells and bombs. I wish I could leave school. Aren't you excited? (*Close-up of* CATHY – *her blank unexcitement*) I bet Dad'll let you keep at least a pound of that. You'll have to buy me a present. And you'll get paid even more when you're

twenty-one, and that's only two years. Mr Carson our history teacher says the war might go on for years and years. I might be able to work there too ...

3 Tony's Parents' House Living-room Early Evening

TONY *is* CATHY's *boyfriend: about twenty-one, thin, nervous, studious, myopic.*

TONY's MOTHER *is busy about the conservatory, off the living-room.*

Silence, a sense of constraint.

TONY. And how's the piano-playing?
CATHY. All right, I suppose.
TONY. Still working on the same piece?
CATHY. It's beginning to seem rather pointless. I'm really doing it to pass the time.
TONY. Till the factory opens ...

Close-up of CATHY.

TONY's MOTHER. There isn't a girl in town who isn't going to be working in that factory. I don't know what the boys are going to do if it blows up with you all inside it.

Laughing, she goes out into the garden.

TONY *and* CATHY *laugh politely till she has gone.*

TONY *takes* CATHY's *hand.*

TONY. I've got some news. It's a secret though.
CATHY. Oh.
TONY. I might be working for ... Intelligence.
CATHY. A spy!
TONY. Well, no. I'll just be someone in an office, helping with

the files. That's at first anyway. I'll be in London, at Senate House.

CATHY. I thought your Dad wanted you to join the army.

TONY. Strictly speaking I *will* be in the army. I wouldn't be much use to them as a soldier, and they're looking for people who are good at modern languages. They'll have to find me digs – somewhere in Bloomsbury I expect.

CATHY. Perhaps I could do something like that. I'm quite good at French and my German . . .

TONY. Well, yes. You could, but I doubt if they will take girls.

CATHY. I suppose not.

TONY. I might have to sign the Official Secrets Act.

CATHY (*moving away*). Yes.

TONY. Of course, I won't be much more than an office boy at first, a kind of secretary.

CATHY. You don't even know how to type.

TONY. You could teach me. You know what, you could even teach me how to cook. I'll need to know if I'm going to live away from home.

CATHY. And I could teach you something about office procedure.

TONY. Jolly good idea.

CATHY. And all about card index systems.

TONY. Yes, that's it.

CATHY. And coach you a little in French and German.

TONY. Ha ha. I know what you're thinking.

CATHY. Do you?

TONY. I'm sure I'll be able to get away most weekends, you needn't worry on that score. We'll be together as much as it's possible in a war, far more so in fact now that I'm not going to be cannon fodder. And when we do see each other we'll have an awful lot to talk about.

CATHY. You'll be able to tell me all about the intelligence system.

TONY. Well, I suppose once I've signed the Official . . .

CATHY. And I shall be able to tell you all about working in a munitions factory.

CATHY *moves away towards the conservatory.*

TONY. Yes ... Look Cathy, you're being awfully sarcastic about everything. I thought you'd be delighted at my news.

CATHY. I'm quite bowled over for you.

TONY. There you go again. What's the matter with you? Seriously, Cathy, what's the matter with you?

4 Bus Shelter
Later the Same Evening

CATHY *sits on a bench in a bus shelter, lost in thought.*

Another passenger stands nearby.

The sound of aircraft overhead.

CATHY *stands to watch them, but they cannot be seen.*

She returns to the bench.

A bus pulls up. The other passenger gets on.

CATHY *remains.*

5 The Raines' Living-room
Same Time

MR *and* MRS RAINE *are in their fifties.*

MRS RAINE, *a comfortable, slightly ineffectual woman, knits.*

MR RAINE, *an accountant with a family firm, sits staring at the clock, a newspaper resting on his lap.*

6 Country Road

CATHY *walks along a country road.*

She stops by a gate and stares across a field.

7 The Raines' Living-room Twenty Minutes Later

The sound of a key turning in a lock.

MR RAINE. Here she is ... Well?

CATHY (*pausing*). I don't want a scene, Dad.

MR RAINE. Where are you going, Cathy?

CATHY. I'm going up to bed.

MR RAINE. It's a quarter to ten. The last bus should have got you in half an hour ago. We've been waiting, and I think we deserve an explanation.

MRS RAINE. Did you miss the bus, dear?

CATHY. No, I felt like walking, so I walked.

MR RAINE. Walked?

CATHY. Yes, walked.

MR RAINE. Did you have your fare?

MRS RAINE. Of course she had her fare.

CATHY. Yes, I did. I felt like walking, that's all.

MRS RAINE. You walked all that way by yourself?

CATHY. It's only one mile, Mum, and I wanted to be by myself.

MR RAINE. You walked a mile in the dark by yourself?

CATHY (*rising note of hysteria*). You're getting the picture now. I wanted to walk, I wanted to be by myself and I wanted to be in the dark. (*Deliberately*) I walked by myself in the dark.

Pause.

MR RAINE. Why?

CATHY. I don't want a scene. I'm sorry if you were worried, I really am. Now I'm going to bed.

MR RAINE. No you are not, young lady. Not until I've heard what you were doing out alone in the dark.

CATHY. I was thinking.

MR RAINE. Thinking? What about?

CATHY. About myself, and about the war.

MR RAINE. Ha! Planning it all out were you?

CATHY. That's right, Dad. Trying to plan it out for myself.

MR RAINE. She'll be telephoning the Prime Minister in the morning to tell him what to do.

CATHY (*deliberately*). I said, I was trying to plan it out for myself.

MRS RAINE (*conciliatory*). She was thinking about starting work at the factory.

MR RAINE. And will you be doing any more 'thinking' in the near future?

CATHY. I expect so.

MR RAINE. Perhaps next time you will give your less intellectually gifted parents a little advance warning so they do not sit up worrying about you.

CATHY. I was half an hour late home and I've said sorry. I'll say it again. Sorry. Sorry. Sorry.

MRS RAINE. Cathy!

MR RAINE. You know, anything might have happened to you out there. A young girl out alone in the dark.

CATHY. Anything might have happened, but it didn't. It never does.

8 Living-room
Following Morning

CATHY *plays her Fantasia* K475. *She falters and stands impatiently.*

9 Office
An Hour Later

A dingy office in the munitions factory. Women queueing in the corridor outside are being interviewed here at three desks.

CLERK. And father's occupation?

CATHY. Accountant.

CLERK. Mother's maiden name?

CATHY (*pause*). I can't remember.

CLERK. Find out and come and tell me next week, before you start work. Now sign these where I've marked a cross. You don't need to read them, you know.

CATHY. I want to know what I'm signing.

CLERK. It is simply an acceptance of the conditions of your employment. There really isn't time.

CATHY. If there isn't time then I won't sign.

CLERK (*standing*). Very well. Take the papers. Read them, sign them and join the end of the queue. Next girl, please.

10 Corridor

A middle-aged woman takes CATHY's *place.*

Outside in the corridor there is a queue of women of all ages. CATHY *walks its length, reading the papers in her hand.*

She leans against the wall at the end of the queue.

The mixed sound of the women's voices is harsh in the acoustics of the bare corridor.

CATHY *folds the papers into her handbag and leaves the queue.*

11 The Raines' Living-room Late Afternoon

CATHY *is at the piano,* TONY *is in the armchair normally used by* CATHY'*s father.*

CATHY *plays a stormy passage from* K475 — *a series of wild runs.*

TONY *reads* The Times.

CATHY *breaks off mid-passage. Exhilarated, she crosses to the fireplace and regards* TONY.

TONY (*without conviction*). That was terribly good.

CATHY. You weren't even listening.

TONY. Yes I was. It's coming on very well.

CATHY. Tell me what's in today's paper.

TONY. Do you really want to know?

CATHY (*laughing*). Of course I really want to know. What sort of question is that?

TONY. If you really want to know ... the 51st Highland Division has been forced to surrender. Eight thousand men have been taken prisoner. There will probably be more evacuations, like Dunkirk, but on a smaller scale. And ... today, the Germans are expected to enter Paris.

CATHY. Isn't it exciting!

TONY Exciting?

CATHY. Yes.

TONY. It isn't a game you know, Cathy. We've suffered a huge military defeat and the Germans are probably about to invade us.

CATHY. I know that, Tony.

TONY. I get the impression you are more interested in practising the piano than in anything else. I mean, you've hardly spoken a word to me all afternoon. You don't seem to be taking the war very seriously, Cathy.

CATHY. Oh yes I am ...

As she speaks, CATHY *crosses the room and sits on the arm of* TONY's *chair.*

Ever since Dunkirk I've been waking very early in the morning like a seven-year-old on Christmas Day. For the first few seconds I don't know why it is, I just know that something very important is in the air. Then I remember the war. The Germans are about to invade us. We might have to fight for our lives, everything is about to change forever. This morning I woke up just before dawn and couldn't get back to sleep. I got dressed and went for a walk. It's funny . . . but I felt ecstatic. I kept stopping to touch things – a fence, a lamp post, a letter box – everything I put my hands on felt more real than ever before. The sun came up and everything I looked at was vivid . . . and precise . . . objects somehow looked like themselves only more so. Does that make any sense?
I walked to the park and when I got there I burst out laughing at the trees – they looked so green, so ridiculously green.

TONY *is still bemused, and a little overwhelmed.*

I felt very happy, and at the same time very restless.
I thought, I want to be *doing* something, I want to be in a room with charts and maps where decisions are made,
I want to hold in my hand lists of how many lorries and tanks we've got, or fly a plane or fire a gun. I want to learn something difficult.

The front door slams.

They hear MR RAINE *in the hallway.*

And then, as the day wears on, my exhilaration wears off.

Cut to MR RAINE's *point of view. He hangs up his hat, changes into his slippers.*

CATHY's *voice.* Everything is much the same really. People are talking about tea rationing and how much you can get up at the munitions factory, not about fighting in the streets.

(*Back to* CATHY) Or what it would be like to live under the Nazis.

A pause.

MR RAINE *has entered the room. He closes the piano lid and stands near his chair.*

TONY *edges guiltily out of it and stands across the room, but* CATHY *continues to sit on the arm.*

MR RAINE *hovers, waiting for her to move.*

What do you think, Dad?

MR RAINE. Human nature being what it is I should imagine that life would not be so very different as some people would have us believe. Governments change, but people basically don't.

CATHY. The Germans would censor all the newspapers.

MR RAINE. The Government does that now.

TONY. But that's because of the war, Mr Raine.

MR RAINE. Do you really believe that the newspapers told the truth before the war? That's very naïve if I may say so.

CATHY. Anyone who spoke out against the Germans would be shot or put in prison.

MR RAINE. Only last month the Home Secretary put several politicians in prison without trial.

TONY. But they were Fascists, Mr Raine!

MR RAINE. That's what the newspapers call them.

CATHY. But they were!

MR RAINE. I'm surprised at you both. Tony has a degree from the University College at Hull and Cathy, you've got Higher School Certificate with three distinctions. Do you seriously believe that a British government, even in peace time, would allow a group to go free who genuinely threatened the perpetuation of the present system?

CATHY. If people voted for that group then the government would be replaced by them.

MR RAINE. My dear girl! The newspapers and the wireless are there to make sure that people vote in the right way. If people started voting for the wrong things, then they'd soon put an end to voting. You can take my word for that.

CATHY. So why don't we invite the Germans here to come and run things for us. That's what you want, isn't it? You could put on your black shirt and wave to them from the front garden.

MR RAINE. If you don't want to discuss this sensibly, Cathy, you may as well leave the room.

CATHY. *Heil*, Hitler!

CATHY *leaves, slamming the door behind her.*

MR RAINE *sits down in the vacated chair.*

TONY *stands in front of him, lingering awkwardly.*

MR RAINE *tut-tuts and shakes his head.*

Pause.

MR RAINE. One thing is for sure, Tony. A lot of people are going to die in this war. You might be one of them. Now Moseley would have kept us out of the war, and with honour.

TONY. I don't think—

MR RAINE. Eighteen months ago you were a pacifist and a socialist, like all your chums at the University. Now you can't wait to be killing Germans . . . for Winston Churchill.

TONY. The circumstances—

MR RAINE. Could it be that you've been reading too many newspapers?

TONY. The circumstances have changed, Mr Raine. We have to forget our differ—

MR RAINE. Ha! That's a good one. And do you think these differences will go away while we forget them?

TONY. Well . . .

MR RAINE. Yes, that's right. You'd better run along and find her. See if you can calm her down.

TONY *backs out of the room.*

MR RAINE *sits.*

12 The Raines' Kitchen
Following Morning

CATHY, ANNA *and* MRS RAINE *sit round the table polishing the silver.*

CATHY *sits slightly apart, remote.*

ANNA. But Gooseberry says, 'Aha, so it was you, Moorehead, I should have guessed.' And Keith says, 'Please sir, it was the caretaker', but Gooseberry doesn't hear him. He grabs him by the arm and pulls him to—

MRS RAINE. Anna, you must concentrate on what you're doing.

ANNA. Pulls him out to the front, so the whole class—

CATHY. Why don't you shut up for a minute or two.

MRS RAINE. Cathy!

CATHY. I've heard this story twenty times already.

ANNA. You liar!

CATHY (*mimicking*). So the whole class starts to chant 'Caretaker, caretaker, caretaker,' and old Gooseberry holds up his hand and then . . .

ANNA. Someone else told you.

CATHY. Each time you tell it you change it. First time round there were just four or five of you chanting. Now it's the whole class.

ANNA. That's a filthy lie!

MRS RAINE. Anna!

ANNA. It's just because she's in a bad mood. She's always in a bad mood.

CATHY. Hah!

MRS RAINE. Will you two please stop bickering. Anna, do this fork again.

CATHY. Anyway, Anna, I wanted you to be quiet for a moment so that I could tell you something important.

ANNA. I don't care.

CATHY. Very well.

Pause.

CATHY and MRS RAINE *go on polishing.*

ANNA *waits.*

ANNA. All right, what is it then? And it had better be important.

CATHY (*pleased with herself*). I'm going to join the army.

Pause one beat.

ANNA *sniggers.*

MRS RAINE. The army? You?

CATHY. The ATS. I'm going to be a soldier.

CATHY *salutes.*

ANNA. You wouldn't dare. She's joking, Mum.

CATHY. No, I'm not. I've been to the Labour exchange, and I'm going back there next week for medicals.

ANNA *giggles.*

MRS RAINE. But Cathy. You know very well it's out of the question.

CATHY. No, tell me why, Mum.

MRS RAINE (*with difficulty*). You've had a good home and a decent education.

CATHY *waits. Mood dangerous.*

Everything we could afford, you've had. Piano lessons, holidays in Germany.

CATHY *sets down the spoon she had been polishing.*

You're a . . . I know this isn't a fashionable word with people of your age, but you're a respectable girl, Cathy.

CATHY. What's that got to do with it?

ANNA *covers her face and laughs.*

MRS RAINE. You know very well what I'm talking about, don't you. Last week I was at the bus station sitting across from three or four soldiers, nicely turned out boys. Two ATS came by and just smiled right at those young boys, bold as anything. And when they'd gone do you know what the soldiers called them? 'Scum of the earth,' that's what they said. 'There goes the scum of the earth.'

CATHY. I see.

MRS RAINE. The ATS is not a place for respectable young girls.

A pause while CATHY *decides not to lose her temper.*

She picks up her spoon and smiles.

13 Frinton Green Sward
   Same Afternoon

CATHY *and* TONY *carry a deck-chair each along the Green Sward. Blustery weather, a strong wind.* TONY *is a couple of steps behind* CATHY.

Long shot first.

TONY. I cannot believe it.

CATHY. What?

TONY. I cannot believe that you really want to do a thing like this, Cathy.

CATHY. Can't you?

TONY. I suppose you realize that this is more or less the end for us. I mean, apart from the kind of company you are going to be keeping and the kind of temptations that are going to be put in your way ...

CATHY. What do you mean by that?

CATHY *has stopped at the top of the grassy slope down to the beach. The way is barred by barbed wire, skull and cross-bone signs warning of mines, etc.*

TONY. And what about your parents? Have you considered *their* feelings?

Fade to bottom of the slope.

TONY *has caught* CATHY *up. He is irritable after handling his deck-chair in a strong wind.*

TONY. . . . and that's precisely the attitude of your average Tommy, fast and loose. You know what everybody says about the ATS.

CATHY *is remote, looking round for a way down to the beach.*

CATHY. Oh yes . . .

TONY. Apart from all that, the chances of us getting leave at the same time are pretty slim. Who knows where you'll be posted.

CATHY (*turning to face* TONY). No, I don't think we'll be seeing much of each other for a bit. But then, as you keep saying yourself, this isn't a time to be thinking of ourselves, is it?

CATHY *sits down.*

TONY. But you don't have to go to the other extreme and be so totally selfish. You had important war work to go to . . .

CATHY. Important war work!

TONY *remains standing, deck-chair under his arm, and lectures her.*

TONY. Of course it's important. More important than the ATS. You can't fight a war without munitions. Your pay would have been very good. Between us we could have put something away, and we should have been able to go on seeing each other. Now that's all finished.

CATHY. Would you do it?

TONY *starts to put up his deck-chair.*

TONY. Do what?

CATHY. Work in the munitions factory until the war is over.

TONY *is having the classic difficulties erecting his deck-chair. He works at it throughout the following.*

TONY. They're not taking on unskilled men, and anyway—

CATHY. Never mind that. What if they were, you're so anxious to go on seeing me, why don't you stay here while

I join the army. (*Mimicking*) I'm sure I'd be able to get away most weekends. We'd be together as much as it is possible in a war ...

TONY (*still struggling*). You're being perfectly ridiculous.

CATHY. And when we did see each other we'd have so much to talk about. Why do you think your war is so much more important than mine?

In exasperation TONY *lets his chair fall flat. He straightens up.*

TONY. For goodness sake, Cathy, you're talking as if I've been given the chance to run the war. I'm going to be little more than an office boy. Most of us are going to have to do boring jobs, there's no way round it. You seem to be taking it as a personal insult that no one has offered you your control centre – your room full of maps and your lists of lorries. Who do you think you are? What's so special about you?

TONY *picks up his chair, erects it carefully and sits.*

CATHY *and* TONY *stare out to sea.*

14 Tony's Parents' House Living-room Evening of the Same Day

A sulky silence, then:

TONY. What's happened to you?

CATHY. What do you mean?

TONY. You've become so hard about everything. You should have seen your face when we were talking just now. You looked so ... well ... mean, Cathy. The ATS is full of women like that, I've seen them in town, rowdy ... awfully aggressive in fact, not like women at all. And those dreadful uniforms. There's something horrible about seeing a whole lot of women in uniform, something sinister. They don't look like women at all, they're more like ... like ...

CATHY. Men?

TONY. No, ants. They're just like ants.

15 Mr and Mrs Raine's Bedroom Early Morning

MR RAINE *is preparing to go to work. He stands in front of a dressing-table. He rubs Brylcreem into his hair violently.*

CATHY *knocks at the half-open door and enters. She is smartly dressed.*

CATHY. I thought I'd come up to say goodbye.

MR RAINE *does not turn round.*

CATHY's *tone is slightly desperate, hoping for reconciliation.*

He combs his hair, knots his tie.

My train leaves at nine ... there's four of us travelling together to the camp. They gave us rail warrants after the medicals ... I expect it will take hours to get there, you know what the trains are like now. So ... er ... I'll write as soon as I ... I expect it will be very strange at first, being with so many people ... So, goodbye Dad. Goodbye ... Dad?

CATHY *leaves the room, closing the door quietly.*

16 The Raines' Hallway
Early Morning

CATHY *embraces her sister and her mother wordlessly.*

17 Railway Station

CATHY *walks on to the platform, suitcase in hand.*

She stands at the end of the platform.

18 Officers' Mess
Day

Twenty male army officers sit in armchairs facing a low dais on which there is a lectern.

A high-ranking ATS officer addresses the men.

ATS OFFICER. Many of you have expressed doubts about women soldiers, and all of you will shortly have women under your command. It is almost certain that the government will be granting the ATS equal military rights with men in the army – the woman soldier is to be a fact of life to which you must adapt yourselves, and these few notes should be of some use to you. Working Conditions: It should be realized that women are not good at standing

19 Country Road
Day

A group of ATS recruits which includes CATHY *sets off, dressed in PT kit, on a cross-country run.*

ATS OFFICER (*voice over*). The fatigue engendered by standing has a bad effect upon their capacity to take in instructions and will induce inattention, fidgeting, boredom. All instruction classes should be planned to alternate standing and seated classes, and where possible women waiting their turn should not just be 'stood at ease' but allowed to sit down.

CATHY *runs along a narrow country road, long, easy, rhythmic strides.*

CATHY's *new friend,* MARY, *is a little way behind her.*

MARY (*shouting*). Cathy! Wait for me!

CATHY, *over her shoulder, without stopping.*

CATHY. No! I'm going to beat you all.

20 Officers' Mess
Day

We look at the faces of the male officers, relaxed, bored.

ATS OFFICER. *Esprit de Corps* and Handling. In order to build up an *esprit de corps* among women – who are normally lacking in community consciousness – enthusiasm must be built up and inspiration supplied; there is very little 'glamour' and less 'colour' in modern army life. Women need a 'thrill' to produce enthusiasm which is the first step towards *esprit de corps*.

21 Canteen Day

A succession of faces at a serving-hatch. ATS privates hand in their trays; ATS orderlies wash up.

ATS OFFICER (*voice over*). This can be given in many ways. The tradition of the army, of the regiment, well told. They must be made to feel they belong by taking part in parades as well as training. It is imperative that the women should feel they are being taken into the confidence of their commanding officer, that he trusts them, *relies* on them. To make them believe this he must actually do so. Many commanding officers will have their misgivings – but the women must not know this.

22 Lawn Day

ATS privates receive map-reading instruction.

CATHY *and* MARY *sit close together.*

23 Officers' Mess
Day

The officers: some restless, some whispering to each other, one at the back reading.

ATS OFFICER. Women will always reciprocate once their trust is given. It is a natural instinct with them to live up to what someone whom they like and respect thinks of them. It should be remembered that 'rumour' plays a bigger part with women than with men. Their capacity for magnifying and altering any rumour which reaches them is incredible. The casual conversation of officers might be overheard, and you should guard against making any criticism or seeming disparagement of the women in training or the rumour will spread that the officers do not believe in the women's capacity and will cause alarm and despondency. In connection with defaulters, a word or two about tears.

24 Barracks
Evening

ATS OFFICER (*voice over*). Tears are natural with some women, and are frequently perfectly genuine. Take no notice, but if it continues, a brisk word or two of a bracing nature usually stops them. There is another type which becomes deeply depressed and may turn hysterical. Send these out of the room and put a woman NCO in charge. When they have recovered have them back and begin again. The worst type is the woman who can turn tears on and off, according to the effect gained. With these an attitude of slightly amused detachment will work best, as it gets under their self-esteem. But do not let them get away with it because they cry. Women have a fairly good instinct for justice and respect it, even at their own expense.

The dormitory presents a scene of domesticity and preoccupation. Some girls are fully dressed, but without ties or jackets. Others are in their underwear, and some are in regulation pyjamas and dressing-gowns.

A variety of activities, a gentle buzz of conversation, occasional laughter. A table has been covered with an army blanket and is being used as an ironing-board. One girl does another's hair. Letter-writing, card-playing, kit-polishing.

CATHY *sits on the edge of her bed, in pyjamas, massaging her calves.* MARY *sits on the chair, showing* CATHY *home photographs.*

The ATS SERGEANT *enters unseen and stands by the doorway. She is small and severe. She is noticed by the girls nearest her. Silence spreads through the room slowly. The* SERGEANT *stands waiting.*

Finally the only sound comes from two girls at the far end of the hut in deep conversation. They become aware of the silence around them and break off.

The room freezes.

SERGEANT. Open your lockers and stand to attention by your beds!

Scramble and hubbub.

Quiet!

Two untidy lines are at last formed. The SERGEANT *advances slowly between the lines. A snort of laughter.*

Another sound and I'll have you standing here till breakfast.

The SERGEANT *kicks shoes out of her path.*

I've never seen anything like it in all my life! This hut is a shambles. A bloody shambles!

She darts forward and throws the contents of one locker across the floor.

A pigsty!

She tips out another locker, and another, and another, in manic rage.

You're not humans. You're disgusting pigs!

The girls watch in amazement as the SERGEANT *proceeds like a whirlwind down the line.*

She comes to rest, breathless. Total chaos around her.

You've got ten minutes to put this hut in order. And I mean order. The lights are going out in ten minutes.
RECRUIT. Please, Miss . . .
SERGEANT (*wheeling*). What was that?
RECRUIT (*holding up her hand*). Excuse me, Miss . . .
SERGEANT. Permission to speak, Sgt.
RECRUIT. Permission to speak, Sgt.
SERGEANT. Permission not granted.
RECRUIT. But Miss . . .
SERGEANT (*screams*). Sergeant!
RECRUIT (*whispers*). Sergeant.
SERGEANT. You have nine minutes. I want this hut immaculate, do you understand? Anyone not ready for lights out when I return will be in serious trouble.

She leaves. For a moment no one moves.

SECOND RECRUIT (*retrieving her smashed portrait of Fred Astaire*). Look what she's done. Look what she's done!

In total silence the girls set about clearing up the mess.

25 Officers' Mess Day

ATS OFFICER. The *esprit de corps* of women is largely built upon respect, faith and love of the cause or of the show. Once given, their trust is hard to shake. It will pull them through most hardships, because they will never wish to let down the person to whom they owe that faith and trust. Thank you for your attention, gentlemen. Now I will hand you back to Colonel Cooper.

26 Drilling Shed
A Few Weeks Later

From their appearance and drill it should be apparent that the recruits are near the end of their basic training.

The line of recruits stands at attention while a male SERGEANT-MAJOR *inspects them.*

SERGEANT-MAJOR. Squad ... squad ... shun!

They come to attention.

An ATS SERGEANT-MAJOR *stands deferentially to one side.*

He passes down the line, making ritual adjustments here and there, followed by the ATS SERGEANT-MAJOR.

SERGEANT-MAJOR. C platoon. Stand ... at ease.

ATS SERGEANT-MAJOR (*distributing lists*). You have twenty hours to study the lists and choose your task in life. Watch the noticeboard for details and times of aptitude tests. Don't choose nothing your mother wouldn't like.

SERGEANT-MAJOR. Squad ... dismiss.

27 Canteen
The Same Day. Evening

CATHY *and* MARY *sit alone at a table, staring at their lists. We are aware of other girls on other tables doing likewise.*

MARY (*South London*). But Cath. You don't know what you're letting yourself in for. Special operator, it could mean anything. In fact, it sounds to me like a kind of spy or something.

CATHY. I'd like that. 'Cathy, our special operator behind enemy lines.'

MARY. Or something to do with aeroplanes.

CATHY. Wonderful.

MARY. Don't be daft. They're bloody dangerous, Cath. You wouldn't catch me going up in one. You don't want to be a special operator. Choose something we can both do. That way we can stick together.

CATHY. Like a cook.

MARY. That's it, something nice like that.

CATHY. I could have stayed at home and cooked every day for my Dad.

MARY. A driver then.

CATHY. Boring. Driving other people around who are doing the interesting things.

MARY. But all through basic training we've said we'd stick together, Cath.

CATHY. So you'll have to be a special operator too.

MARY. You're joking mate. Catch me being special. It's all I can do to keep ordinary.

CATHY. Well, I'm going to be special and so are you. It's probably pastry cook in an officers' mess anyway.

CATHY *and* MARY *are on their way out of the canteen. Near the door is a piano.*

CATHY *pauses by it, tempted.*

MARY. Can you play?

CATHY. Well ...

Standing, she stretches her hands over the opening chord of her piece and plays it.

28 Huts
Six Months Later. Dawn

The chord is sustained.

We make out a cluster of low huts in the grounds of a country house, a government interception station.

A motor bike starts, comes towards us and recedes.

From one of the huts, which show no light through their black-out blinds, the sound of a typewriter.

29 Inside One of the Huts

Arranged along the length of the hut, two rows of four tables. At each table sit two ATS wireless operators wearing headphones. All listen, some write.

At one end of the hut a male sergeant-major of the Royal Signals sits alone reading a report.

To one side of the sergeant-major, an ATS GIRL types.

In the wireless hut we move in closer on the operators. We hear faint, rapid Morse signals through their headphones. A sense of total exhaustion.

We find CATHY at one of the tables. Unlike most of the other operators, she is not operating on a fixed frequency. She turns her tuner through a range of frequencies. We hear what she hears through her headphones: static, warbling noises, then a faint Morse signal which she passes and returns to immediately.

She begins to print out neatly on a pad groups of five-letter words, each totally unintelligible as, for example, WZZRQ.

The signal strengthens and then fades.

CATHY *leaves gaps when she cannot hear clearly.*

The message ends. CATHY *notes the time in an appropriate box on the signal pad and the frequency and her name.*

She begins to turn her dial through the frequencies again and puts the message in her out-tray.

The ATS GIRL *collects it.*

ATS GIRL. Almost half way, love.

The message is folded into a container and placed in one of those suction tubes they used to have in department stores. The tube leads to the teleprinter room. Here messages are taken from the canister and copied on to the teleprinter.

A DISPATCH-RIDER *enters. He picks up the night's signals and puts them in his bag. He exchanges small talk with one of the operators (male) and leaves.*

Back in the wireless hut, a door opens and two orderlies carry in a tea urn. The sudden blast of cold air makes everyone shiver.

The orderlies take a large mug of tea to each operator. No one stops work.

CATHY *sips her tea and turns her dial.*

30 Outside the Radio Hut End of Shift

CATHY *walks across the grass with the other girls from her shift, towards the dormitory.*

The sound of squeals and cries.

31 Inside the Dormitory

A gang of ATS have chased and caught SARAH.

As CATHY *enters they are carrying* SARAH *towards the washroom. But she lashes out with her feet and they have to set her down on the floor.*

There they overpower her again and edge her towards the washroom. For everyone but SARAH *a sense of fun coupled with a determination to teach her a lesson.*

We find MARY *amongst the girls.*

AD LIB. . . . Get her . . . Got her . . . Hold her legs, put me down . . . I shall report you, etc.

MARY (*shouting*). Come on, Cathy. Give us a hand.

CATHY (*approaching*). What are you doing to Sarah?

MARY. We're gonna teach her some basic hygiene, aren't we, girls? If she can't behave clean, she can at least learn to keep herself clean.

FIRST ATS GIRL. She hasn't had a bath in a month. Little stinker.

SARAH. How dare you.

MARY. What a pong.

SECOND ATS GIRL. She'd have a different man every night if she had half the chance.

FIRST ATS GIRL. She only come back the other night with her knickers rolled up in her hand.

SARAH. Let me go!

MARY. Lift her up! It's bath time, little stinker.

CATHY *watches as they carry* SARAH *into the washroom and dump her fully dressed in a full bath. They throw underclothes and stockings in after her.*

SARAH. You . . . you bastards.

SECOND ATS GIRL. Listen to that language.

FIRST ATS GIRL. She's not getting out of there till she's scrubbed that lot clean.

SARAH *attempts to get out of the bath and they push her back.*
She weeps with anger.

SARAH. You bastards, you bastards, you bastards.

Cries of ooh and aah from the girls.

32 Dormitory
A Couple of Minutes Later

CATHY *lies on her bunk, still dressed in heavy overcoat. Too numbed*
by tiredness to move.

The girls file back into the dormitory from the washroom. SARAH's
cries can still be heard.

MARY *sits down by* CATHY's *bed.*

MARY. Now I see why they call it the graveyard shift.

33 Dormitory
Midnight

CATHY *is in bed asleep.*

An ATS LANCE CORPORAL *bends down to wake her.*

ATS LANCE CORPORAL. Raine ... Raine. Your shift's on.

She moves on to wake others.

34 Dormitory
   A Few Minutes Later

CATHY, *in greatcoat, pushes open the door and steps into the night*

35 Corridor
   Late Morning

The unit's noticeboard is in a long corridor.

CATHY, MARY *and a couple of other ATS are clustered round it.*

MARY (*with excitement*). Listen to this! It's from Bletchley: 'On the 3rd December, between 23.59 hours and 08.00 hours, messages were intercepted by your station that were of in ... in-est-im-able value to High Command. Keep up the good work.' Cathy, that was yours, the graveyard shift. It might even have been you what wrote it down.

CATHY (*excited but controlled*). Inestimable value ... what could it have been about? You know, they should tell us more about what we're doing. Copying down those letters eight hours a day ...

MARY *steers* CATHY *away from the noticeboard and along the corridor.*

MARY. Don't start on that again. You'll get a bad name for yourself.

CATHY. I'd just like to know more, that's all. It would make the job less frustrating. Between 23.59 hours and 08.00 hours – they could tell us more than that if they wanted to. They treat us like little girls ... (*laughing*) those big boys.

36 Outside One of the Huts Following Morning

A DISPATCH-RIDER — *the one we saw earlier* — *is tinkering with his motor bike. His fingers are cold and therefore clumsy. He is about* CATHY's *age, and a private. He swears under his breath.*

We become aware that we are watching him from CATHY's *point of view, several feet off, and unseen by him.*

CATHY. You must get jolly cold riding that thing in this weather.

DISPATCH-RIDER. What?

CATHY. I said, it must get very cold ...

DISPATCH-RIDER. Bloody freezin'.

CATHY. I hear you go off towards the end of our shift, first thing in the morning. I always wait for the sound of your bike because then I know we don't have long to go.

DISPATCH-RIDER (*smiles*). Ah ...

Pause, awkward.

CATHY. Do you have to go very far?

DISPATCH-RIDER. BP and back. 'Bout hundred and twenty mile.

CATHY. BP?

DISPATCH-RIDER. Bletchley Park.

CATHY. Of course. Bletchley's the centre of it all, isn't it. What's it like?

DISPATCH-RIDER. You know what they got there?

CATHY. No.

DISPATCH-RIDER. Girls. Thousands and thousands of girls. There's never been so many girls in one place. After the war no one'll believe it.

CATHY. And no men?

DISPATCH-RIDER. Well, officers ... and all the blokes from Cambridge University, in civvies like.

CATHY. They must be in great demand.

DISPATCH-RIDER (*laughing*). Not them, you must have heard
  about them.
CATHY. No, I haven't.
DISPATCH-RIDER (*embarrassed*). Half of them ... are, you
  know ...
CATHY (*still unsure*). Oh ...

The DISPATCH-RIDER *covers his embarrassment by pretending to be
absorbed in his bike.*

CATHY *hovers, awkwardly.*

  I expect I'll bump into you again
DISPATCH-RIDER (*vaguely*). Yeah.
CATHY. For a chat.

The DISPATCH-RIDER *nods and pokes at his bike.*

CATHY's *pride is damaged.*

  It must be boring for you, with all your thousands of girls.

She turns on her heel and walks quickly away. The DISPATCH-
RIDER *watches her go, surprised.*

37 Radio Hut
     Night

CATHY *and all the other ATS at work.*

CATHY *is taking down a signal, printing quickly in neat capitals.*

*A faint warbling sound grows in volume. It becomes harder and
harder to hear the Morse.*

The girl next to CATHY *dozes off. The sergeant notices her and sends
the typist to wake her up.*

38 A Public House

A country pub some miles from the camp. A fairly respectable place.

The saloon, a few farmers and a few junior officers (male) are drinking at the bar.

Conversation is at a low murmur.

We are aware that something is up; the publican is glancing uneasily, and a little aggressively, into one corner of the room.

A couple of customers glance that way too, rather amused. A few nods and winks.

From the customers' point of view, we see CATHY *and* MARY *at a table with half a pint of beer each, talking. They are in uniform.*

They huddle into their conversation. Throughout it we should be aware, as they are not, of the mounting hostility towards them as unaccompanied women.

We come in on the girls' conversation at a point where it has broken down into spluttering but restrained laughter.

MARY. . . . Oh Cath, it sounds daft, but he's got muscles where no one else is meant to have them . . .
CATHY. How do you know?
MARY. I met 'im at the seaside last summer, didn't I?
CATHY. That's right.
MARY. Listen, his arms can't even hang straight. He's out here.
CATHY. King Kong.
MARY. Corporal Kong!

More laughter.

The PUBLICAN, *polishing a glass slowly, shakes his head.*

Oh he's sweet really . . . tiny little waist he's got and (*whispering*) hair growing all over his back.
CATHY. Perhaps you *should* marry him then.
MARY. Oh Cath! I couldn't really. I went out with him once,

only once, honest. Seven months ago, and we didn't even kiss. We held hands at the bus station, but we didn't say nothing.

CATHY. You made a big impression.

MARY. It's because his regiment's going abroad, that's the only reason he wrote to me. He just wants to marry someone before he goes. I'm not being mean, am I?

CATHY. Course you're not. And you shouldn't feel guilty about it either. That's the trouble, you say no to them and they're miserable about it, and make you feel it's all your fault. Or you're friendly towards them right from the start and they think you're loose and disgusting.

MARY. Exactly my way of thinking, Cath.

CATHY. What they want is for you to say no for a bit, and then say yes so they can think they've won you over. They want you to be exactly how they imagine you.

MARY. They're the delicate flowers really . . .

More laughter, then a pause.

CATHY *glances towards the men at the bar, who look away.*

CATHY (*serious now*). Listen, Mary, you mustn't tell anyone what I'm about to tell you now.

MARY. Course not.

CATHY. Two or three night ago I copied down one of the messages I'd picked up on the radio and smuggled it out of the hut . . .

MARY. Cath! Why?

CATHY. Keep your voice down. It sounds stupid I know, but I wanted to have a crack at breaking the code myself.

MARY. You're bonkers.

CATHY. I know a bit of German, see. I knew if I could break the code I would understand what it was all about.

MARY. They'd court-martial you if they found out.

CATHY. I know. And I knew I wouldn't be able to break the code. I didn't know where to begin. But I needed to try it for myself. I keep thinking about it. I'm sure the whole thing is much bigger and more important than we'll ever know, Mary.

MARY. We're not meant to be talking about this, here or anywhere.

CATHY. I know that, but if I don't talk about it, just once, to you, I think I'll go mad. We already know there are two other interception stations from the girls who've been posted there. There might be dozens of stations, all sending messages back to Bletchley, by teleprinter and motor bike. If the codes are being broken that means that they know everything the Germans are saying to each other, everything the Germans are going to do.

MARY. We ought to change the subject.

CATHY. They can't hear us. It's so frustrating doing a job and not knowing what the job is for. Sometimes I think it's complete nonsense, like polishing your boots every night, and other times I think we might be involved in one of the most important jobs of the war.

MARY. You're getting it all out of proportion, Cath ...

CATHY. All of us girls know nothing, and a few of the men know something.

MARY. Well I'm quite happy knowing nothing, thank you very much.

CATHY. They probably think women can't keep secrets ...

MARY. Cath! He's coming over to us.

CATHY. What?

The PUBLICAN looms.

PUBLICAN. Perhaps you young ladies are waiting for someone you know.

CATHY *and* MARY *together (innocent, baffled).* No ...

PUBLICAN. I thought you weren't. (*Pointing at their empty glasses*) Waiting for someone to buy you a drink then, are you?

MARY. No. We was just talking.

PUBLICAN. Talking!

CATHY (*to* MARY). We haven't been buying drinks. I'll get them. It's my turn.

CATHY *stands.*

PUBLICAN. I'm not serving you.

CATHY. Not serving us? Why not?

MARY. We weren't doing nothing, were we, Cath?

PUBLICAN. Sorry. You'll have to go.

CATHY. What?

PUBLICAN. Out you get. I've got my other customers to think of. Come on. This isn't the kind of place you think it is.

CATHY. We're not going.

PUBLICAN. Yes you are, young lady. This is a respectable pub, not a place where you can hang around and wait to be picked up.

CATHY. You dare touch me!

MARY. Come on, Cath. Let's go

PUBLICAN. Do what your friend says. Out! Or I'll call the military police.

CATHY *refuses to move.*

The PUBLICAN *hauls her by the lapels.*

CATHY (*furious*). Get off me! Get off me!

The PUBLICAN *slaps* CATHY'*s face, the cure for hysteria.*

PUBLICAN. Calm down.

He lets her go.

CATHY *brings her knee up sharply into the publican's groin, a well aimed blow that connects with a sickening thud.*

The PUBLICAN *jack-knifes and walks backwards slowly.*

CATHY *raises two hands to her face utterly horrified.*

The PUBLICAN *collapses on to his backside and stares at* CATHY *in wonderment and agony.*

MARY. Oh Cath!

39 Office Day

The small, bare office of the COMMANDING OFFICER *of the interception station. The* CO *is a major (male).*

CATHY *is marched in by an escort.*

She comes to attention and salutes.

The CO *watches her from behind his desk.*

He consults some notes.

An ATS *officer is present.*

CO. You were asked to leave a public house and you refused to go. You assaulted the publican and caused him grievous bodily harm. Is that correct?

CATHY. Yes sir.

CO. Intolerable. I've had some violent, crude, drunken men under my command who start fights on a Saturday night and get themselves thrown out of pubs. And I've come down on them heavily for it too. But never, never have I had a soldier attacking a publican. The *publican*, Raine. Are you attempting to get yourself discharged from the army?

CATHY. No sir.

CO. Assaulting a publican. I'm not sure I wouldn't rate that more serious than rape, wouldn't you? (*Loud*) Well, wouldn't you?

CATHY (*whisper*). Yes sir.

CO. What was that?

CATHY. Yes sir.

Pause.

CO. Have you anything to say about this?

CATHY. No sir.

CO. Good, because I don't particularly want to hear about it. Your work is satisfactory, so is your turn-out. But your attitude ... your supervisor isn't too happy with your attitude to your work. Perhaps you're not up to the pressure. I could court-martial you for this, Raine, but I won't. I'm getting rid of you instead. You'll be confined to barracks for a month on orderly duties. By then your posting to Bletchley will have come through.

CATHY. Sir?

CO. Yes, general duties at Bletchley. This goes down on your record, Raine, a black mark against you. Another wrong move and you'll be in very serious trouble.

CATHY. Yes sir. Thank you sir.

CO. Now get out of my sight.

40 In the Grounds of the Interception Station Morning

CATHY *and* MARY *in greatcoats embrace tightly, wordlessly.*

We see MARY's *face.*

Pulling away we see CATHY's *kit bag on the ground, packed and ready.*

41 The Raines' House. Living-room Afternoon

CATHY *has returned home while everyone else is out.*

She looks at herself in the mirror; adjusts her uniform.

She approaches the piano and tries to lift the lid. But it is locked.

The front door slams and ANNA *runs into the room.*

CATHY *stands and they embrace wildly.*

ANNA *is in school uniform.*

ANNA. We only got your letter yesterday. I thought today
would never end. I've been watching the clock at the front
of the class all afternoon. Cathy! You look so different.
CATHY. How?
ANNA. You look bigger, much taller.
CATHY. They make us stand up properly. (*Pulling at* ANNA)
Come on. Straighten that back. Chin up. Feel your full
height!
ANNA. Geroff! You're only a private anyway. You can't push
me around.

They laugh and hug each other again.

42 Dining-room
Evening

*The dining-table is laid as for a special occasion, with the best
crockery.*

MR *and* MRS RAINE, CATHY, ANNA, TONY.

CATHY *is in uniform*, TONY *is dressed in Civil Servant's dark blue
suit.*

We have the impression that TONY *has been holding forth for some
time.*

TONY. Of course, what people refuse to understand is that the
Underground stations are death-traps.
MR RAINE (*pouring wine*). You've told us a great deal about
London, Tony, but precious little about what you're
doing . . .
TONY. Well, actually I've been jolly lucky. I've been attached
to the Ministry of Aircraft Production and fast-streamed.
MR RAINE. Well done.

ANNA (*admiring*). What do you have to do?

TONY. I've been helping to write posters.

MRS RAINE. Let's hear one of yours then. I might have seen it.

TONY. Well, I'm not sure I can remember . . .

ANNA. Come on, Tony.

TONY *hesitates, waiting for* CATHY's *support.*

She does not meet his eye.

TONY. There's one from a series called 'Radio Bulletin'. It goes: 'A bomber over Norway . . . a bomber over Norway, gaping hole in the floor, pilot's cabin roof gone, tried desperately to get home. All the maps had blown away. The radio was damaged and very shaky but the operator sent out faint SOS signals for ninety minutes. Only one of them was heard. It was enough . . . Hobbling home, propellers bent, one useless engine, no charts, pilot half frozen, they made landfall at the Shetlands and found lights and welcome waiting. Their success, their confidence, their safety, they all depend on you.'

TONY *has spoken this with an intensity that brings it to bathos.*
A short silence follows.

CATHY. Very good, isn't it, Mum.

MRS RAINE. I don't think I've seen that one.

MR RAINE. Hmm . . .

TONY. Of course, I didn't write it myself, I *helped* write it.

MR RAINE. And what about you, Cathy. How exactly are you helping to defeat the wicked Germans? What does that badge mean?

CATHY. I means I'm in Signals. I'm a wireless operator, or at least (*this unheard*) I was . . .

TONY. That's interesting. Have they trained you to send Morse code?

CATHY. I'm not allowed to say.

MR RAINE. Not allowed! That's a good one.

CATHY. I've signed the Official Secrets Act. I can't tell you what I do . . . what I've been doing . . . without breaking the law.

MR RAINE. She's back here a couple of hours and she's already at her airs and graces. You're that important already are you, *Private* Raine, that they've given you secret work to do.

CATHY. That's right, Dad, most secret.

MR RAINE. And you can't tell us civilians in case *we* tell the Germans.

CATHY. Exactly, Dad.

MR RAINE (*dropping the sarcasm*). You've been away several months now. Your mother's missed you terribly.

MRS RAINE. Well I wouldn't . . .

MR RAINE. No, it's not true, she's missed you terribly. I think we deserve at least a brief explanation from you about what you've been up to.

CATHY. I'm sorry. I can't tell you.

MR RAINE (*standing up, sulky*). Well, wonderful when we haven't seen you in so long to have so much to talk about. I'll have my tea in the other room, Mother, when you're ready.

He leaves.

CATHY (*not moved*). Oh dear.

MRS RAINE. He's been so looking *forward* to you coming home.

TONY. Is there really nothing at all you can tell us about yourself, Cathy?

CATHY. W150050 Auxiliary Raine, C.

43 One Week Later. Bletchley Park Officers' Mess. Morning

CATHY *has been assigned to general mess duties, acting as a dog's-body to the officers' mess, which is in the main building. The mess is used principally, but not exclusively, by civilians – university mathematicians.*

She is laboriously polishing the floor.

The mess is deserted except for one young officer who sits reading the newspaper.

A wireless plays military band music and this gives way to a talk. Its tone is one of patronizing intimacy and bluff inanity.

We follow CATHY's *vigorous movements as she listens.*

WIRELESS. Let's get a few things straight. First understand, as many people don't seem to, that the WRNS, the WAAFs, and the ATS haven't been built up for fun, or to ensure that young women are as inconvenienced as much as young men, or as a substitute for hockey clubs, but (*deliberately*) because we are desperately short of man-power. In modern warfare an enormous non-combatant force is needed to maintain men in the front line. In the British army for example, as in the German army, one-third of the men spend their time supplying, repairing and administering the other two-thirds. Now, a lot of this administrative work can't be done by women, but an awful lot can! In the days of the women's suffrage campaign, a favourite argument of the opponents of the enfranchisement of women was that women should not be allowed to vote because they were incapable of defending their country. Nothing would have surprised these people more than the competent, goodhearted way their grand-daughters have proved them wrong. One of the most useful spheres for women in the services is cooking. As the war progresses the number of meals they cook each day for His Majesty's armed forces has risen to millions. Even more impressive is the . . .

CATHY *turns the wireless off.*

OFFICER. I say! What's going on? I was listening to that.
CATHY. Sorry sir. I thought it might be getting on your nerves.
OFFICER. Bloody cheek.

CATHY *turns the wireless on and leaves.*

The OFFICER *goes on reading.*

We look at CATHY's *gleaming floor.*

WIRELESS. .... and the Prime Minister himself, Mr Winston Churchill, having been blessed with three daughters, has been able to contribute one to each of the services. Henceforward, as our colossal war machine gets under way, no skilled person is to do what can be done by an unskilled person, and no man is to do what can be done by a woman ...

44 Kitchen Evening

In a small kitchen along the corridor from the mess CATHY *prepares to carry in a tray of coffee cups and coffee.*

In the background we hear animated male conversation and laughter.

While the water heats on the small stove, CATHY *mops the floor.*

45 Mess Evening

Several young men languish in armchairs.

Two play chess.

In one corner a grand piano.

A couple of young army officers are here too, but they sit more formally, reading newspapers and keeping out of the conversation.

The atmosphere among the young mathematicians is one of after-dinner self-regard and genuine seriousness.

CATHY, *making coffee in the next room, overhears.*

CLARK. There are of course the theological objections, you know.

MATTHEWS. Where's that coffee?

CLARK. I mean, if you were to tell a clergyman you had a machine over in the other hut that could think, I'm sure he'd take a pretty dim view.

TURNER. Theological arguments are not very impressive as far as I'm concerned. In Galileo's day . . .

MATTHEWS. Aha, Galileo!

TURNER. Matthews, why don't you keep your mouth shut?

MATTHEWS. I'm sorry, Turner old friend. Waiting for coffee makes me hysterical. Carry on, carry on.

TURNER. In Galileo's day, Joshua 10:13, 'And the sun stood still, and hasted not to go down about the whole day' and Psalm 105, 'He laid the foundations of the earth, that it should not move at any time', were considered an adequate refutation of the Copernican theory.

MATTHEWS. He knows his Bible.

TURNER. With what we know now, Matthews, such an argument appears futile. At the time, however, it made a quite different impression.

CLARK. Very well, but the burden of proof is really yours to show us that a machine is capable of thinking.

MATTHEWS Exactly.

TURNER. The trouble is one tends to get bogged down in definitions of 'machine' and 'think'. A better way would be to think of the problem in terms of a game which I've called the 'imitation game'.

MATTHEWS. Can we play it?

TURNER. Well almost. There are three players. A man, a woman and an interrogator who can be of either sex. The interrogator stays in a room apart from the other two but connected by a teleprinter. His aim is to find out which of the two is the man, and which is the woman. The object of the man is to try and cause the interrogator to make the wrong identification, while the woman's purpose is to help the interrogator.

CATHY *enters unseen, stands by the door with the tray and listens.*

Probably the best strategy for the woman is to answer truthfully, and she can add things like 'Don't listen to him! I'm the woman', but there's not much point because the man can make the same kind of remarks.

CATHY *advances very quietly towards the group to hear clearly. We watch from her point of view.*

Now, the question is this. What will happen when a machine takes the part of the man in the game? Will the interrogator decide wrongly as often when the game is played like this as he does when the game is played with a man and a woman?

MATTHEWS. Wait a minute, Turner!

TURNER. What is it?

MATTHEWS. Shouldn't you first establish whether the woman can think? It's not something one can take for granted, you know.

General laughter. Even the military are amused.

The group becomes aware of CATHY standing behind them with the tray and the laughter subsides, but without embarrassment.

CATHY *moves forward and begins to serve out the coffee.*

TURNER (*sour*). Very amusing. Perhaps, Matthews, the subject would interest you more if the imitation game were played with little boys.

The military retire behind their newspapers.

MATTHEWS. Yes, indeed, Turner. I'm sure I could count on you to arrange it.

A silence.

CATHY *moves from one to the other. Ad libbed coffee business.*

CLARK. How will this new form of the problem make it easier?

CATHY *is standing in front of TURNER.*

As he replies, their eyes meet briefly.

TURNER. Let's talk about it later. I'll show you ... did I hear something?

From down the corridor, a muffled shouting. Everyone in the room turns expectantly.

Another young mathematician, SMITH, runs into the room.

SMITH. Red's up! Red's up! In less than one hour. You're all needed. Turner, it was your new menu.

Great hubbub. TURNER is congratulated.

The chess players make a hurried note of the state of play.

They all leave. The room is suddenly silent. Only the young officers remain.

CATHY, *bewildered, stares at the untouched coffee cups arranged around the room.*

She begins to gather them up.

OFFICER (*to the other, holding out his paper*). Swop?

46 Phone Box

CATHY *dials.*

It should be apparent that both CATHY and MARY are relatively unfamiliar with telephone conversations. They call out rather than speak. They start sentences at the same time. They are excited by the sound of the other's voice, but they find they have little to say. This is a friendship based on huddled intimacy.

Stay with CATHY.

CATHY. Mary ... Mary, is that you? Mary?
MARY. I said, you'll have to shout. I can't hear a thing.

CATHY. Mary!
MARY. Cathy! I can't believe it's you, you sound different.

At the same time as CATHY:

What's it like?
CATHY. Do I? You sound the same.
MARY. What? What's the weather like?
CATHY. It's been raining.

At the same time as MARY:

I hate it here.

47 Corridor. Main Building Morning

CATHY *walks alone, towards camera, along a deserted corridor.*

48 Dormitory Same Morning

CATHY *drops torn pieces of a letter into a wastepaper basket.*

49 Dormitory
Same Morning

CATHY *sits on the end of her bed.*

50 Mess
Same Morning

CATHY *has come to the piano. She puts down her duster and lifts the lid.*

She glances round to make sure no one is about.

She presses one key and admires the quality of the sound.

She sits down and by an effort of memory begins to play her piece.

As she plays, TURNER *enters the mess from a door behind her, sits down and opens a file on his lap.*

He watches and listens.

Finally CATHY's *memory of the piece runs out and she falters.*

TURNER. I think you'll find the music inside the piano stool.

CATHY *stands. Ruffled, slightly annoyed.*

Do go on. It's one of my favourite pieces.

CATHY *picks up her duster and carries on as before.*

CATHY. I don't think other ranks are meant to play it.
TURNER. Mozart's only for officers?
CATHY. I meant this piano.

CATHY *cleans out a fireplace.*

TURNER. Do you like your work?

CATHY *ignores him.*

    Why don't you answer?

CATHY. I don't like being patronized.

TURNER. I see. And you think this work is beneath you.

CATHY. I didn't say that.

TURNER (*mimicking*). Everyone has to do their bit.

CATHY. Quite.

TURNER. And as long as you do it well ...

CATHY *stands.*

CATHY. Look, if you're transferred next week from breaking codes to washing dishes, then I'll come and listen to what you have to say about doing your bit well.

TURNER. Don't get angry. How do you know what I do?

CATHY. I guessed. Now I've got to get on with my bit.

CATHY *goes to leave.*

TURNER. I say.

CATHY. What?

TURNER *crosses room and stands in front of her.*

TURNER. My name's John Turner, King's College Cambridge.

CATHY. How do you do. Private Raine, Frinton.

TURNER. Come on, stop being so tragic for one minute.

CATHY *relaxes, offers him her hand.*

CATHY. Cathy Raine.

TURNER *keeps hold of her hand.*

TURNER. May I call you Cathy?

51 Corridor. Main Building Day

CATHY *is delivering a heavy Imperial typewriter.*

She stops at a door. A sign reads, 'NO UNAUTHORIZED PERSONNEL'.

CATHY *knocks, waits and then opens the door. She carries the typewriter in and rests it on a desk.*

The room fascinates her. She cannot quite leave it. She advances a pace and looks around.

It is cluttered. Charts, maps and technical drawings are pinned to the walls. Books and files are piled high on two or three desks. In one corner a teleprinter clatters intermittently. There is a radio receiver.

When CATHY *takes another step she discovers an* OFFICER *squatting on the floor staring intently at technical drawings, a pencil in one hand.*

CATHY *gives a little cry of surprise and startles him out of his concentration.*

OFFICER. What the bloody hell are you doing in here?

CATHY (*coming to attention and saluting*). Delivering a typewriter, sir, as requested.

OFFICER. Typewriter? Didn't you see the notice on the door?

CATHY. I knocked . . .

OFFICER. So you thought you'd come in and have a good look round.

CATHY. I thought—

OFFICER. You don't think. If no one is here you go away and wait until there is. Do you understand? No unauthorized personnel.

CATHY. Yes sir.

OFFICER. What's your name?

CATHY. Raine, sir.

OFFICER. Right. Now get out of here Private Raine and take that bloody typewriter with you.

CATHY. But—

OFFICER. Get out! Understand? Out! Out! Out!

The OFFICER *drives* CATHY *out.*

She stumbles, with the typewriter, backwards out of the room.

As soon as she is out, the OFFICER *slams the door shut hard on her.*

A key turns in the lock.

52 Corridor. Main Building Two Minutes Later

CATHY *staggers on down the corridor with the typewriter.*

She meets TURNER *coming the other way.*

TURNER (*friendly, bemused*). Hello there . . .

CATHY *ignores him furiously.*

TURNER *pushes open an adjacent door marked* 'STRICTLY
AUTHORIZED PERSONNEL ONLY'.

The increase in volume of machine noise causes CATHY *to turn.
Intrigued despite herself she watches him disappear.*

*There is a room beyond the one he has entered: the door is ajar,
electronic equipment can be seen, glowing valves, oscilloscopes, etc.*

A colleague of TURNER'S *sees* CATHY *watching and slams the door.*

53 Mess
After Lunch

Several officers and civilians.

Desultory chatter.

A mathematician throws a paper dart.

54 Small Kitchen
A Few Minutes Later

CATHY *is washing up coffee cups.*

TURNER *appears in the doorway.*

TURNER. Hard at it, then.

CATHY. Yes, clean cups and saucers might set the Germans back, don't you think?

TURNER. Shall I give you a hand? Together we could really surprise the enemy.

CATHY. No, I don't want you to.

She moves a tea-towel out of his reach.

TURNER. You know, I think you're a rather difficult person.

CATHY. You think the kitchen skivvy should be an easy person.

TURNER. And you deliberately misunderstand me. Why are you so prickly?

CATHY. Why are you so interested?

TURNER. I like difficult, prickly people. They're awfully intriguing.

CATHY. Just like difficult codes.

TURNER. There you go again. D'you know. I once read that a lady should never stoop to sarcasm.

CATHY. Well, I'm only an Auxiliary.

TURNER. As you keep pointing out.

CATHY *softens at this. She gives* TURNER *the tea-towel.*

CATHY. I don't mind at all being an Auxiliary. I mind spending all my time doing silly little jobs like this when there's a war and I could be doing something useful.

TURNER. Why not apply to be trained in something.

CATHY. I was a special operator ...

TURNER. At one of the interception stations?

CATHY. Yes, but they moved me on.

TURNER. What did you do wrong?

CATHY. I ... I assaulted a publican.

TURNER (*admiring*). I say. Was the beer flat?

They both laugh.

CATHY. It was a terrible thing to do. I shouldn't laugh about it.

TURNER. And now this is your punishment. Bottlewasher.

CATHY. Partly it's a punishment. Partly it's what being in the ATS is all about. Simple repetitive jobs, backing up the men.

TURNER (*glancing at his watch*). At least you're safe, Cathy. The idea of women at the front lines or up in airplanes shooting each other's pretty legs off is appalling, don't you think?

CLARK *puts his head round the door.*

CLARK. Yellow's up, John.

TURNER. Look, I must dash. Yellow's up.

CATHY. Yellow?

TURNER. You will come and have tea with me in my rooms on your next afternoon off, won't you.

CATHY. I'm not sure ...

TURNER. Don't be a stuffed shirt. I'm not an officer. Anyway, it's lapsang sou chong, courtesy of King's College Cambridge. You can't refuse, can you?

He smiles and leaves.

CATHY (*to herself*). No.

55 Turner's Rooms
Two Days Later

TURNER's *rooms consist of study/living-room with doorway into bedroom. A gas fire hisses.*

CATHY *sits on the edge of an armchair, slightly uneasy.*

TURNER *sets down a tray of tea things.*

TURNER. Would you like to pour?
CATHY. No.
TURNER. I thought you might like to be mother.
CATHY. I'd rather wait till the war was over.

They laugh, both a little nervously.

TURNER *pours. The cup that he passes to* CATHY *rattles in its saucer.*

You're very nervy.
TURNER. Oh, sorry. Tip the slops back in this cup. Yes, I expect I work too hard. But we're not allowed to talk about that. Tell me about your family. I suspect you're an only child.
CATHY. No, I've got a younger sister. Why should you think that?
TURNER. You're rather solitary, and quick to defend yourself. And I was an only child – I thought we might have something in common there. I was brought up by my mother. My father was a District Commissioner in Ceylon but my mother couldn't stick it, she came home to England to have me. She's a very forceful lady, quite frightening really, and very gifted . . .
CATHY. What at?
TURNER. Well . . . she's rather good at organizing people, particularly me, and she's not bad at the harpsichord either. She sits a horse very well, as they used to say, and she's something of a crack shot with a bow and arrow, and she's won quite a few trophies at tournaments and that sort of thing.

CATHY. She does sound a bit frightening. Aren't you scared of her?

TURNER (*laughing*). I was a bit, I suppose. Being at Bletchley has rather put me beyond her reach. Do you know, if she came in here now and found me drinking tea with a private from the ATS she'd be outraged, outraged beyond belief. She's a bit of a snob you know.

A pause.

CATHY *is uncertain how to take this.*

CATHY. Would you tell her to mind her own business?

TURNER. Yes, well, I'd have to be tactful of course ... now what about your family. You've escaped Frinton, your father and your fiancé and you're still browned off?

CATHY. Yes, I am.

TURNER. A lot of people say that the ATS uniform is rather drab, but I think it looks marvellous on you anyhow.

CATHY. That's consolation. You look stunning in your grey flannels.

They laugh, TURNER *very uncertainly.*

TURNER. I get the feeling, when I'm talking to you, that you're very angry about something.

CATHY. Let's talk about the war. You're probably the best person to ask. Do you think the Germans still have plans to invade us, or do you think they've gone east for good?

TURNER. Are you angry?

CATHY. Not with you, so answer my question.

TURNER. On one condition.

CATHY. Yes?

TURNER. That you let me hold your hand.

CATHY *proffers her hand graciously.*

TURNER *clambers round the small table between them, kneels on the floor by* CATHY's *chair and takes her hand.*

In the exchange that follows they become increasingly aware of each other.

There. The Germans have elaborate plans for the invasion of Great Britain, but they are so heavily committed in the east that they are in no position to implement them.

CATHY. But that's exactly what the newspapers say.

TURNER. Then for once you can believe what you read. Now tell me about your fiancé ...

CATHY. What about the Americans? Do you think they'll come in?

TURNER. Who knows? But if they don't it might be very difficult to bring the war to any kind of conclusion in the next ten years.

CATHY. I heard someone say that on the radio.

TURNER. So did I.

CATHY. What about the resistance movement in France? Is it true that the government doesn't take it very seriously?

TURNER. Cathy, you are extraordinarily beautiful.

A shocked pause.

CATHY *squeezes* TURNER's *hand.*

He kisses her. She returns the kiss warmly.

They breathe in short gasps.

CATHY. I can hear your heart. Or is it mine.

TURNER (*whispers*). Cathy ... you ... if we ...

Pause.

CATHY (*whispers*). Yes.

Pause.

TURNER (*whispers*). In the bedroom.

CATHY. Yes.

56 Turner's Bedroom

CATHY *and* TURNER *get into bed with all their underwear on and lie facing each other.*

CATHY. It's cold.
TURNER. I'll light the fire.
CATHY. No, it will get warmer.

CATHY *shudders.*

TURNER. Are my hands cold.
CATHY. Yes.
TURNER. Sorry.
CATHY. It's all right.
TURNER. Cathy, are you ... is this your first ...
CATHY. Yes, it's my first time.
TURNER. You don't mind me asking?
CATHY. No, of course not.

CATHY *smiles slightly mischievously.*

   What about you?
TURNER. What me? (*Lying*) It's not ... it isn't really my first
   time ...
CATHY. That's good. You know exactly what to do then.
TURNER. Well ...

CATHY *kisses him.*

CATHY. You know all the secrets.

She cuddles against him.

57 Turner's Bedroom
Later

Late afternoon semi-darkness.

TURNER *lies apart, as far as it is possible in a single bed.*

He gets out of bed suddenly and begins to dress furiously.

CATHY. What are you doing? Where are you going? . . .
Please don't be upset. It doesn't matter.

TURNER. It doesn't matter! My God, you've got a nerve.
No doubt you'll be telling all your friends.

CATHY. I don't understand.

TURNER. I'm sure you don't! Do you know what you are?
(*Approaching the bed*) You're a . . . do you know what you
are? . . . Your first time! You must be enjoying this. It's
working out exactly the way you planned it.

CATHY. No.

TURNER (*mimicking*). No . . . You wanted to humiliate me and
you succeeded. You hate your own job and you're jealous
of me for mine. You wanted to even up the score . . .

CATHY. No!

TURNER. 'You know all the secrets' . . , You vindictive little
bitch.

CATHY. I don't understand. I don't understand what you're
talking about.

TURNER *leaves, slamming the door.*

58 Same Room
Twenty Minutes Later

Shivering from the cold, CATHY *washes her face at the handbasin
and begins to get dressed.*

59 Turner's Living-room
Five Minutes Later

Fully dressed, CATHY *sits on the edge of the settee and waits for* TURNER *to return. She warms herself by the gas fire.*

She notices on a table a small pile of files. She picks one up and reads the words, 'TOP SECRET'. *She hesitates and then opens it. She begins to read.*

She carries all the files to the settee and continues to read. We glimpse something of the contents.

There is a brief knock on the door. It opens and MATTHEWS *enters.*

MATTHEWS. Turner? Oh I'm sorry ... I ... What are you doing in here?

He crosses the room rapidly.

CATHY *stares.*

MATTHEWS. What are you doing with these? (*Mounting panic*) Who said you could read these? (*Stepping backwards*) Don't move, do you hear me. Don't move.

MATTHEWS *walks backwards to the door and shouts down the corridor.*

Corporal! Corporal! Yes you, and that other man. Come here quickly. Quickly man!

MATTHEWS *ushers a corporal and a private (males) into the room.*

CATHY *still has a file open on her lap.*

Now you two are going to stand guard over her till I return, do you understand? (*Gathering up the files*) She's not to move, and you're not to take your eyes off her. Is that clear? My God!

MATTHEWS *runs from the room.*

The corporal looks at CATHY *quizzically.*

She stares back, expressionless.

60 Small Cell. Guardroom Day

CATHY *stands to attention by her bed.*

Apart from a bucket, there is no other furniture in the room.

A COLONEL – *portly, avuncular* – *enters carrying papers.*

An orderly sets out a folding chair near CATHY'S *bed. The* COLONEL *lowers himself into it.*

CATHY *continues to stand to attention while the* COLONEL *opens the file.*

The orderly leaves, locking the door behind him.

COLONEL. Sit down, Cathy.

CATHY *sits down on the edge of the bed, facing the* COLONEL.

He glances through some papers and sighs.

(*with resignation*). This business has gone on too long. It's time we brought it to a conclusion. Cathy, you know more about Ultra than any other woman alive. You've worked in an interception station and you know that side of it, and you've had access to two secret files here and goodness knows what else. In your own statement you said that you read about the German Enigma machines and that you've understood how important our code-breaking operation is to the conduct of the war. You also seemed to have read something of the command structure of Ultra. At the same time . . . (*referring to file*) I have a report from a senior intelligence officer saying that he caught you snooping in his office, I have Turner's report which says you used your

... charms to wheedle information out of him. We've found a scrap of paper in a wastepaper basket near your bed with the words 'Station X' on it in your handwriting. You say it was a letter to a friend which you tore up, and I'm even prepared to believe you. We discover that you spent holidays in Germany before the war, that you speak reasonable German, and that your father was a paid-up member of the British Union of Fascists till 1937. Cathy, we are quite satisfied that you are not a spy, but (*laying his hand on* CATHY's *shoulder*) how can we possibly set you free? We can't. Ultra is too important. We're prepared to shoot innocent people to protect the Ultra secret, let alone lock them up. Since you know what's at stake, I know you'll understand. Turner asked me to give you this. He's in hot water for having those files in his room, but then, he's indispensable.

CATHY *takes the parcel without curiosity.*

CATHY *speaks hesitantly. She has been thinking about this.*

CATHY. ... He thought it was terrible, the idea of women shooting at each other. Shooting each other's pretty little legs off. It is terrifying. It terrifies me because I would hate to lose my legs. But it terrifies men for a different reason ... you know, on the anti-aircraft units the ATS girls are never allowed to fire the guns. Their job is to work the range-finder. If the girls fired the guns as well as the boys ... if girls fired guns, and women generals planned the battles ... then the men would feel there was no ... morality to war, they would have no one to fight for, nowhere to leave their ... consciences ... war would appear to them as savage and as pointless as it really is. The men want the woman to stay out of the fighting so they can give it meaning. As long as we're on the outside and give our support and don't kill, women make the war just possible ... something the men can feel tough about. (*Determined, unhesitant*) But I'm withdrawing my support.

COLONEL (*chuckles*). Well it hardly matters because we're going to keep you locked up. (*Leaning forward, confidential, paternal. Hand on her hand*) Do you know what Fascism is, Cathy? Do you want to see us overrun by the Germans?

CATHY (*furious*). Take your hands off me! Did I say I wanted us to be overrun by Germans? Is that what you think I've been saying?

COLONEL *stands.*

CATHY *stands too, angry and pleading.*

When we went to bed, it didn't matter that he couldn't ... I didn't care, I really didn't care. I liked him. He didn't have to be efficient and brilliant at everything ... I liked him more ... But he couldn't bear to appear weak before me. He just couldn't stand it. Isn't that the same thing? I mean ... as the war. Don't you see, the two ... the two ...

Unable to articulate the connection she has made, CATHY *sits down again, and retreats into frustrated silence.*

The cell door opens. The COLONEL *stands over* CATHY.

COLONEL. You're a very, very silly girl.

The cell door slams shut behind the COLONEL.

CATHY *takes from the paper bag the score of* K475.

She opens it and begins to read.

We read over her shoulder.

Fade in the piece itself, as played by Ivan Moravec.

We watch CATHY *from a jailer's point of view – through the barred window of her cell. She reads the score. The music plays.*

Credits.

Fade out.

Picador

☐	**Paris Peasant**	Louis Aragon	£1.50p
☐	**Great Granny Webster**	Caroline Blackwood	80p
☐	**Making Love: The Picador Book of Erotic Verse**	edited by Alan Bold	£1.95p
☐	**Bury My Heart at Wounded Knee**	Dee Brown	£3.75p
☐	**In Patagonia**	Bruce Chatwin	£2.25p
☐	**I Heard the Owl Call My Name**	Margaret Craven	£1.50p
☐	**The Obstacle Race**	Germaine Greer	£5.95p
☐	**Roots**	Alex Haley	£3.50p
☐	**The Women at the Pump**	Knut Hamsun	£1.95p
☐	**Dispatches**	Michael Herr	£1.95p
☐	**Siddhartha**	Herman Hesse	£1.50p
☐	**Unreliable Memoirs**	Clive James	£1.75p
☐	**The Trial**	Franz Kafka	£1.75p
☐	**One Flew Over the Cuckoo's Nest**	Ken Kesey	£2.50p
☐	**One Hundred Years of Solitude**	Gabriel Garcia Márquez	£2.75p
☐	**The Cement Garden**	Ian McEwan	£1.95p
☐	**C. G. Jung Speaking**	edited by William McGuire	£3.25p
☐	**The Third Policeman**	Flann O'Brien	£1.75p
☐	**Weymouth Sands**	John Cowper Powys	£3.50p
☐	**Midnight's Children**	Salaman Rushdie	£2.95p
☐	**The Best of Saki**	Saki	£1.75p
☐	**The Street of Crocodiles**	Bruno Schulz	£1.25p
☐	**The Bass Saxophone**	Josef Skvorecky	£1.25p
☐	**The Flute-Player**	D. M. Thomas	£2.25p
☐	**The Great Shark Hunt**	Hunter S. Thompson	£3.50p

All these books are available at your local bookshop or newsagent, or can be ordered direct from the publisher. Indicate the number of copies required and fill in the form below   7

....

Name_____
(Block letters please)

Address_____

_____

Send to Pan Books (CS Department), Cavaye Place, London SW10 9PG
Please enclose remittance to the value of the cover price plus:
35p for the first book plus 15p per copy for each additional book ordered
to a maximum charge of £1.25 to cover postage and packing
Applicable only in the UK